PUB W~~ALKS~~

— IN —

Worcestershire

THIRTY CIRCULAR WALKS
AROUND WORCESTERSHIRE INNS

Richard Shurey

COUNTRYSIDE BOOKS
NEWBURY, BERKSHIRE

First Published 1993
Reprinted 1995
© Richard Shurey 1993

COUNTRYSIDE BOOKS
3 Catherine Road
Newbury, Berkshire

ISBN 1 85306 227 8

Cover illustration by Colin Doggett
Photographs and maps by the author

Produced through MRM Associates Ltd., Reading
Typeset by Paragon Typesetters, Queensferry, Clwyd
Printed in England by J. W. Arrowsmith Ltd., Bristol

Contents

Introduction

A fascinating thing about country pubs in this rather stereotyped world is the immense variety available. Town hostelries – invariably modern and rather garish – tend to look much the same but try as you might you cannot find two inns alike in the villages of Worcestershire . . . and what could be better than to work up a thirst on a short walk and then to sample their fare?

Today all pubs welcome the trade that walkers bring, and I don't think that ramblers need reminding to respect the pub where they are guests. Boots often become dirty on rambles along the byways and the mud really does not improve the carpeted lounges – thoughtful walkers treat a good pub as a 'home from home' or perhaps even as a shrine and remove their footwear. Landlords are invariably agreeable to cars being left in their car parks whilst you are walking but do clear up this point before setting out. Likewise check first if you wish to eat food you have brought with you – in the garden and accompanied by drinks from the bar, of course.

Many of us take our dogs on rambles; without exception I found that my Nell was welcome at the pubs. Although her manners are impeccable I fully understood when the rule was that our best friends remain outside. (In any case the law does state that animals – except guide dogs of course – should be excluded from areas where food is served.)

When there are children on the walk do check where they are allowed. Unlike the situation until a year or so ago, many of the pubs really do cater for children with games rooms, reduced meal portions and garden play areas to burn off surplus energy.

I received many suggestions of suitable pubs to visit to compile this book. The difficult choice was initially very wide but the list was reduced to include only those where there was a pleasant circular walk in the area. Others (often equally attractive and welcoming) were cheek by jowl with another in the same village.

I have also aimed to have a good spread of rambles throughout the county. I am sorry if your favourite has been left out.

Finally a little warning. (No, not about the dangers of walking and drinking the excellent pint of real ale that you have earned.) The countryside is continually changing. Although I have recorded the route as accurately as possible when I walked the routes, please do be prepared for changes. Sadly those little worlds of nature – the hedgerows – are still being rooted out, new roads are planned and, more optimistically, footpaths are slowly being improved with new signposts, stiles and waymarks.

The sketch maps are intended to give a simple but accurate idea of the route to be taken. The numbers of the relevant Ordnance Survey maps, in the Landranger 1:50 000 series, are also given. The scale of these is useful for walkers and they show footpaths and bridleways.

Happy walking through Worcestershire – the lovely county of orchards, a gentle landscape of wooded hills, black and white houses, pretty villages and of course some smashing pubs.

Richard Shurey

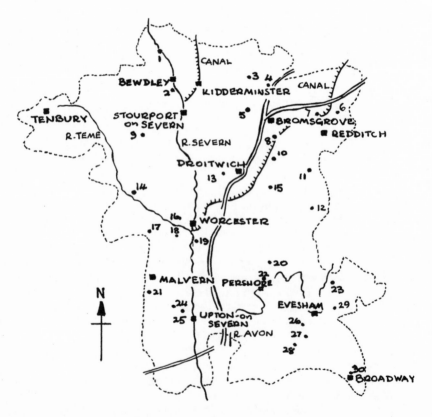

Area map showing locations of the walks.

Arley
The Harbour Inn

A 'harbour inn' not many miles from the centre of the Kingdom? The answer lies in the river Severn – and taxation. When the waterway was an important commercial waterway cargoes were landed at the riverside village of Arley to avoid paying the taxes levied at the town of Bewdley a few miles downstream.

The flower-bedecked pub dates from 1512 and was a coaching inn. The bar (beamed of course) is crammed with interesting and unusual bric-a-brac that would never fail to stimulate lagging conversation. How about stuffed birds, a beam of polished coins, a model of the old (now obsolete) Arley ferry and a poster warning that 'careless talk costs lives' for starters? There is no need for the welcome sign – the convivial atmosphere of the Harbour Inn says it all.

Jacki Bestwick takes a pride in her real ales – Worthington and Bass bitters and M & B Dark Mild. The menu is modest in length but modest in price. I was especially taken by Grandma Batty's Giant Yorkshire Pudding with assorted delicious fillings. Children (allowed in the separate dining room) have their own fare 'all served with chips and beans' and there is always a vegetarian

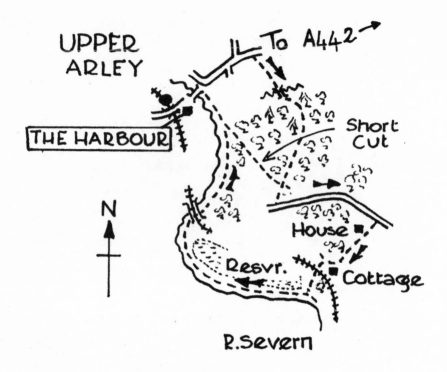

'special'. The inn has variable hours depending on trade and the season.

'Do not forget our garden', said Jacki Bestwick. Rightly – for it is an acre of delight and won a best pub accolade for the area to prove it. There are lovely flower beds, fun play contraptions and an assortment of animals (rabbits, goats, ponies) and birds. Not surprisingly Fido (and my Nell) have to be kept on leads and stay outside.

Telephone: 01299 401204.

How to get there: Turn off the B4194 2½ miles north-west of Bewdley. The lane is signed as a cul-de-sac lane to Arley. The Harbour Inn is at the end of the lane.

Parking: There is a large car park at the back of the inn.

Length of the walk: 3½ miles, but it can be shortened to 1½ miles. OS Map Landranger series 138 Kidderminster and Wyre Forest (GR: SO 766799).

Here is a wonderful walk that you will want to repeat at all seasons as there are woodland paths through trees which constantly change hue. After Eyemore Wood the path descends to the river to pass Trimpley Reservoir. The track back to Arley then hugs the riverbank to go under the cast iron Victoria railway bridge which dates from 1861. (I have lost count of the number of times this spectacular structure has appeared in films and on TV.)

The Walk

If you are at all interested in railways (and who is not interested in real steam trains), before you turn right to the river go left a few steps to the famous Severn Valley railway. To cross the river there is now a utilitarian steel bridge and locals (and us other folk who love traditional things) bemoan the loss a few years ago of the old ferry boat. Over the water keep ahead uphill along the road. Within ¼ mile and just past a junction take a signed bridleway on the right.

Walk along a cart track – banked at first then fenced and through fields to the woods. The track twists a way through trees then crosses a brook. Stay on the main track now climbing steeply to build up that thirst. At a wood yard and meeting of tracks keep ahead. Drop downhill to a crossroads of wide paths. (For the short cut turn right – signed WW.) Stay on the same direction to a lane. Turn left for ¼ mile. Just after the end of the right hand woods a path starts. Go down a dip where tractors pass through a field gate. In a pasture walk near the right hand hedge to a gate to woodlands.

Continue along the wide track to bear right by a cottage to a junction of ways. Turn left to a railway crossing place. Over the tracks and a step stile go left to swing around a reservoir where water from the river is stored to provide an additional supply for Birmingham. When the river Severn is reached follow the pathway to the right. This leads to the footbridge at Arley then it's back to your 'haven' – sorry, your 'Harbour'.

Ribbesford
The Woodman

No one could pretend that this welcoming inn beside the river Severn was pretty – its history is against it. But it is a popular refuge for fishermen and strategically placed for walkers walking through the upland Ribbesford Woods. It has only been a pub for 20 years or so – it was previously a cafe and ice-cream parlour to serve the public swimming pool which was in a woodland glade behind the building (now a caravan site).

John Court in this free house knows which beers to sell with Banks's Bitter, Carling Black Label and Stella Artois as the most popular. The Strongbow cider is also a favourite with walkers. The menu consists of good traditional pub food (including salads) with a special chilli and lasagne for vegetarians. The opening hours are 12 noon to 3 pm and 7 pm to 11 pm but are flexible in this enlightened age.

Children are allowed in the bottom bar and many dogs bring their well-behaved owners to The Woodman – both are allowed in the non-eating areas. There are plenty of benches and tables outside where one can watch the world (and the river) go by.

Telephone: 01299 403288.

How to get there: The Woodman is on the B4194 2 miles south of Bewdley.

Parking: There is a large car park beside the inn.

Length of the walk: 3¼ miles. OS Map Landranger series 138 Kidderminster and Wyre Forest (GR: SO 786732).

There is a puffing climb immediately but as always the reward is a splendid view – this time far over the Severn Valley. Part of the route is along the waymarked Worcestershire Way to Ribbesford where the Normans built a lovely church. The great Tudor mansion nearby was the seat of the Lords Herbert of Cherbury and during the Second World War it was a secret headquarters for General de Gaulle and the Free French.

The Walk
At the back of the inn is an unsigned path which climbs sharply alongside the hedge. Join a forest road (these are Forestry Commission lands) and keep ahead past blackberry bushes with good fruit in season. Pass one junction. A little further the 'road' sweeps right by a meeting of several tracks. Keep the same heading to leave it, now

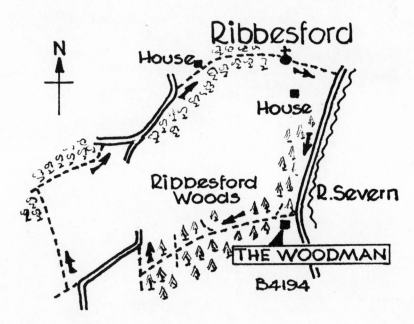

walking along a rocky track. Cross another forest road and maintain the direction still through trees. At a T junction turn right along the wide way to a stile onto a lane.

Turn left for ⅓ mile. The lane goes sharp left. Walk a few steps along a farm drive ahead then turn right to strike out over the sometimes sown field. Nearing the far side of the field aim for the right hand corner of a wood. Maintain the heading now with the elongated wood on your left. In the corner of a field is a waymarked crossroads of paths. Turn right now following the well-signed Worcestershire Way to a lane. Turn right then left at the T junction. Within 300 yards go right along a vehicle track. Follow the waymarked route to Ribbesford church and walk along the drive to the B4194. Follow the river downstream to The Woodman.

Clent
The Vine Inn

Being below the slopes of the lovely tree-clad Clent Hills the 18th century Vine is a very popular pub for walkers although the vine which once climbed to the eaves can now only be seen in pictures. The building was once a mill and the brook still tumbles alongside. For many years beer was brewed here but nowadays Brew XI and Bass Special are served and there is a choice (sweet, medium and dry) in the draught ciders of Blackthorn Sweet and Dry Blackthorn.

The choice of meals is wide, with specials always available (seafoods are good) and excellent snacks. What I especially like though are the modest prices. Meals are taken in the two timbered and beamed bars, busy at times but always comfortable and relaxing. Children are allowed and children's portions served. Dogs on leads and only in the garden please. Opening hours are from 11 am to 3 pm, and 6 pm to 11 pm.

Telephone: 01562 882491.

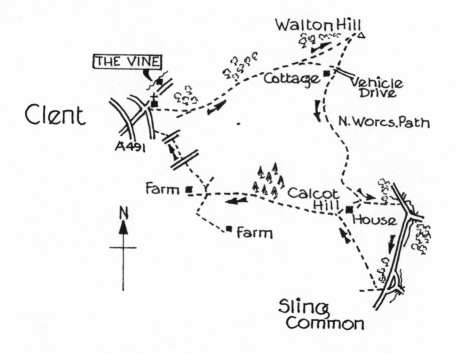

How to get there: Take a lane leading off the A456 at Hagley to Clent village. At the crossroads by the church go along the lane signed to Romsley and the Vine is reached after about 300 yards.

Parking: There is a large car park alongside the pub.

Length of the walk: 3½ miles. OS Map Landranger series 139 Birmingham and surrounding area (GR: SO 930795).

There are some good climbs on the walk to work up a thirst for your visit to this fine inn. Most of the high uplands are owned by the National Trust. The walk starts through the little village of Clent where the red sandstone church with a large clock dates back over 800 years. The barrel-vaulted roof is especially attractive.

The Walk
Out of the car park turn right along the lane to Clent village. At the crossroads turn left. Immediately past the church take a path on the left. The track follows alongside the churchyard to a hill pasture. Cross the field to climb a stile to woods. Follow the clear track to heathlands

14

then to the trig point on the top of Walton Hill – splendid views from here. Somewhat reversing the direction now pick up waymark arrows of the North Worcestershire Path. There is a junction of tracks by a cottage. Still following the waymarks join the vehicle drive left.

Climb a stile on the right and take the arrowed direction to walk alongside a right hand hedge. Climb another stile and soon follow the well-walked path by a new plantation of saplings.

At a signed junction of paths turn left (still the North Worcestershire Path) to go by a waymark post. There is now a descent to a lane. Turn right. Keep ahead at a meeting of lanes. Here there is a pretty lane through trees and bordered by a brook which once powered many of the scythe mills at the village of Belbroughton downstream.

Keep ahead again at the next junction but soon take a vehicle drive on the right – this is also a bridleway. Within a few steps take a signed bridleway by a house on the right. The bridleway goes along a vehicle way and climbs to Calcot Hill. In the 18th century the Lord of the Manor was Richard de Caldcote.

Follow the vehicle drive for about 1¼ miles. Opposite a drive to a farm go over a stile to the field right. Take care as there are two paths here and ours is not arrowed. Go half left to a fence stile by a metal gate. In the next field keep the same heading to a stile to a lane. Cross to the opposite stile. Keep ahead to join a vehicle drive to a lane. Cross to the metal kissing gate and cut off the corner of a meadow to a white wood kissing gate to a lane. Turn right to the centre of Clent village and retrace your steps along the lane to the Vine.

Romsley
The Manchester Inn

Why Manchester, when the city must be 100 miles away, neither Barry Woodward, the lessee, nor the locals could tell me. They all mentioned the affectionate nickname of this pub – 'The Spout' – which nudges the delightful Waseley Hills Country Park. The inn sign depicts a horse trough with water filling from 'the spout'.

The origins of the pub are likewise a little obscure but it was probably built as a hostelry to serve travelling passengers on the main road. The decor is simple but the place has a welcome homely feel and, being adjacent to the North Worcestershire Path, is very popular with walkers who take their drinks and eats in the garden. The public bar is tiled and 'boot-proof' and the open fires are welcoming in wintertime. There is also a restaurant.

The menu range is large and gives good value for money and John (who has been a chef for 25 years) is particularly proud of the fresh (not frozen) cod. There are always daily 'specials' chalked on the board. The real ales supplied are M & B Mild, Brew XI and the locally popular Enville Ale, and there is usually a guest beer available. The hours are 11 am to 3 pm and 6 pm to 11 pm. Meal hours are much the same and negotiable. The house dog is friendly and welcomes other well-behaved friends. There is likewise no firm rule with children – the procedure is to ask.

Telephone: 01562 710242.

How to get there: The pub is on the B4551 1 mile south of Romsley on the right.

Parking: The pub has a large car park on the opposite side of the road.

Length of the walk: 3 miles. OS Map Landranger series 139 Birmingham and surrounding area (GR: SO 963780).

The attraction of this walk is the wonderful country park – part of a range of hills which has created a fine inviolate boundary to the south-west of Birmingham. It is difficult to imagine that one is so close to a large city. The climbs are just right – not too severe but challenging enough to earn a pint at the Manchester Inn.

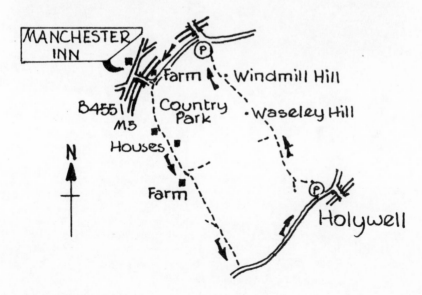

The Walk

From the car park walk a few steps southwards along the B4551. Turn left along the cul-de-sac lane. By a cottage turn right through a metal gate (marked as no entry for vehicles). Follow the way over a road bridge (following North Worcestershire Path signs).

Past a farm the path goes left along a lane. We turn right along a rough farm cart track (signed as a way to Chadwich). The track becomes a footpath. Keep ahead to pass a house. Near a farm maintain the direction over a stile to a field. The farm is now on your right side. Walk straight down the field to a stile into woodlands. These are lovely in all seasons but especially at autumntime. Follow the clear path to a stile to a vehicle drive. This takes us through meadows where cows graze to a lane.

Turn left. The narrow way leads to an area called Holywell – wells were venerated in pre-Christian days and were later taken as places to worship by the Church. Turn left into a car park. Look for a path (North Worcestershire Path signs again) climbing left to National Trust lands. Follow the path alongside low bushes. Drop down to a junction of paths. We keep ahead taking a way over Waseley and Windmill Hills (no mill on the latter now but a toposcope) to the visitor centre of the Country Park (toilets, refreshments, information).

Go along the vehicle drive to a road. Turn left, then left again within a few steps at a junction. This lane goes to the first farm and so retrace your steps over the main road to the B4551 and the Manchester Inn.

Chaddesley Corbett
The Talbot Inn

There have been about thirty licensees of The Talbot Inn from 1800 but I doubt whether any were as enterprising as Rupert and Hilary Boden. Theirs is a pub of which they can be proud with fine drink and food, a cosy and welcoming ambience, and a thought for the family clientele.

Like many rural inns The Talbot (which was identified as Chaddesley's tavern in 1600) was a homebrew house with a simple brewhouse in the backyard of which it is said the beer brewed in the middle of the last century at a gravity of 1060 was the second strongest in England. There are now three bars (serving real ales – Banks's and Marston's as guests) and a restaurant. The decor reflects the old age inn but with discreet modern comforts. Bar meals are served from 11.30 am 'til 2 pm and 6 pm 'til 9 pm. The comprehensive menu is augmented each day with 'specials' chalked on the board, vegetarians being particularly well catered for as Rupert grows his own vegetables – the vegetarian bake is strongly recommended. Opening hours are from 11 am to 3 pm and 6 pm to 11 pm.

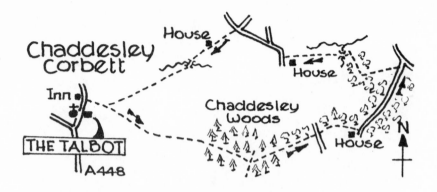

Children are welcome and they especially love the garden with a large grassy expanse and even table tennis (if they have energy after the walk). My collie Nell did not object to being kept on the lead in the pretty garden.

Telephone: 01562 777388.

How to get there: Chaddesley Corbett is just off the A448 (Kidderminster to Bromsgrove road).

Parking: In car park behind the pub.

Length of the walk: 4 miles. OS Map Landranger series 139 Birmingham (GR: SO 892736).

This is an especially fine walk at autumntime as the route is through Chaddesley Woods. This National Nature Reserve has 53 hectares of native oak woodlands which once formed part of the great Royal Forest of Feckenham. There is a short stretch of lane walking and the return to The Talbot is along the valley of the little Hockley Brook. There are no stamina-sapping climbs.

The Walk

Out of the car park turn right along the main street of Chaddesley Corbett. The road is a living museum of domestic architecture with styles of many ages blending delightfully together. Within 200 yards and opposite another inn take a signed path. The cart track leads through fields, then keep ahead along a footpath to a stile to Chaddesley Woods. Maintain the direction to climb to a meeting of several wide tracks.

Go left, then at once right. We follow the yellow arrowed path. (The nearby white arrowed way is The Jubilee Walk which was introduced in 1977 to mark the 25th anniversary of the Queen's accession.) The route is now through trees to a stile to pastureland.

Regain the old direction walking beside left hand woodlands to a lane. Cross directly over. We are again walking through woods to climb a stile by a house. Continue along the drive to a lane. Turn left. Just before a junction take a path over a stile on the left.

Walk through a pasture then over a stile by an orchard. Keep ahead to a wood. Turn right. About 75 yards before a corner the path veers off to the left. Through bushes the path is clear to cross a brook. Climb a stile by a Chaddesley Wood sign. Turn right to a meadow. Walk through the fields to climb a new stile to a lane to the right of a house. Turn right for ⅓ mile. At the second road junction take a path signed down a vehicle drive left. Climb a fence stile before the house. Make for the bridge over the stream in the far left corner of the pasture. Over the water walk over a series of stiles to the outward route. Retrace your steps to The Talbot.

Weatheroak Hill
The Coach and Horses

Phil and Sheila Meads have been at the Coach and Horses for many years and they have worked wonders to retain a basically simple rural cottage-type pub whilst at the same time winning a reputation for good value bar food and adding a modern restaurant which is mellowing into the scene.

Great care is also taken with the beer by Ken the cellarman. He knows a good beer and here he has eight real ales for the beer connoisseur. When I called I found Flowers Original, Boddingtons, Wood's, Burton Festival, Bridge, Old Expensive, Batham, Bishops Finger and Ansell's Mild. The cider drinkers are not forgotten – they can choose between Taunton Traditional and Strongbow. There is a Drinker's Fault Finding Chart by the bar showing symptoms, faults and action to be taken.

The building dates from 1780 and was a favourite inn on the stagecoach route which followed the Romans' Icknield Street southwards from Birmingham. Passengers stayed opposite at the half-timbered building which is now a farmhouse and used the Coach and Horses for their liquid refreshment. It was also the scene of the inquest on Jim Davies, a local bobby killed nearby in 1885, whose murderer Moses Shrimpton was the last man to be hung at Worcester.

There are three bars at the pub where the home-made food served is listed in the comprehensive menu (with specials of the day on a board). The favourite here is gammon and eggs and for all meals children's portions can be obtained. Hours of opening are 11.30 am to 2.30 pm (meals 12 noon to 2 pm) and 5.30 pm to 11 pm (meals 6 pm to 9 pm).

This is a country pub where dogs are part of the way of life. I was told that Fido (and Nell) might be joined by 'a hundred' but I think this may be an exaggeration. There is a large garden with plenty of benches and tables.

Telephone: 01564 823386.

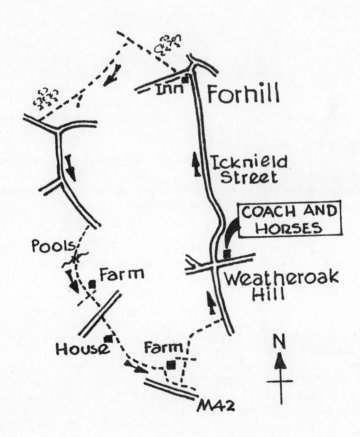

How to get there: The Coach and Horses is situated at Weatheroak Hill (2 miles east of Alvechurch) on the lane between the A441 at Alvechurch and the A435 at Wythall.

Parking: There is a large car park at the side of the pub.

Length of the walk: 4½ miles. OS Map Landranger series 139 Birmingham and surrounding area (GR: SP 057741).

The pub is situated in quite a hilly area so this is a most attractive walk which you will want to repeat at different seasons. The route goes along a narrow squeezed lane which was the old Roman highway – when the wind is blowing you can hear the sound of the legions' feet I'm certain.

The Walk

Coming out of the car park turn right to walk downhill to the crossroads. Turn right along the lane signed Icknield Street. The banked lane climbs past farmsteads to reach Forhill. (There is a picnic site here marking the start of a long distance route – the North Worcestershire Path.) There is also another inn nearby.

Turn left along the lane by the pub but immediately bear off to the right along a vehicle way. Within almost ½ mile take a path over a stile on the left. Follow the path which descends to a lane. Turn left then right at a junction.

Keep ahead at the next junction. Within a ⅓ mile and just before a metal gate climb a stile on the right. In the field walk by the left hand hedge to a stile nudged by a pool. Go over another stile – a waymark arrow directs us over the field to pass between pools. Bear half right to a rough stile to the right of barns. A fenced way now leads to a vehicle drive.

Cross to the opposite stile and go over the field to another onto a road. Turn right then take a signed path left along the drive of Shepherd's Cottage. Walk by buildings to a stile to a field. Keep ahead to another stile. Maintain the heading never far from the left hand border. Nearing a farm climb a new stile right and continue alongside a left fence to a ladder stile. Follow a waymarked path over stiles near the motorway to a signed division of paths. Take the left hand way and cross a house drive then walk through fields (path still way-marked). At the end of two fields after the drive turn 90° right (still by left hand hedge) to a lane. Turn left – this is Icknield Street again and we follow the way of the Romans (and stagecoaches) to the pub.

24

Withybed Green
The Crown Inn

This is a pub which cannot depend on passing trade – unless you count the summertime traffic on the Birmingham and Worcestershire Canal – as it is situated near the end of a cul-de-sac lane. However walkers know of it because the lane leads to some delightful footpaths over gentle hills.

The inn once depended on the canal trade as it was a stop-over for the bargees and horses could be rested and stabled here. The exact age of The Crown Inn as a pub is uncertain but I think we can safely go back to the early years of the last century. There is an ancient fire plaque on the wall to ensure the arrival of a fire appliance if required. Mitchells and Butlers took over the place in 1904 and this brewer's real ales (Brew XI and Mild) are still sold together with Bass and Pedigree. David and Tricia Fisher as lessees offer a limited but mouthwatering menu and the prices are modest. Traditional faggots and mushy peas, and a crusty baguette filled with a tender steak and onions are just the thing for a hungry rambler.

The opening hours are 11 am to 2.30 pm and 6 pm to 11 pm but go a little before closing time to ensure time for meals. The Fishers'

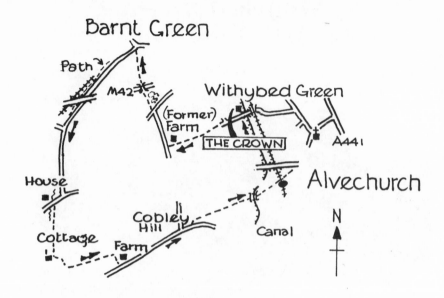

placid Alsation who used to pretend to guard the front entrances has sadly gone but Fido (and my Nell) are still advised to stay outside. Children are allowed into the bars if eating meals but otherwise there are plenty of tables and benches outside.

Telephone: 0121 445 2300.

How to get there: A441 to Alvechurch. From the centre go along Bear Hill. Opposite the church turn down Swan Lane. Within ⅓ mile proceed left – Withybed Lane. The pub is ¼ mile just over the canal bridge.

Parking: The car park is opposite the pub.

Length of the walk: 5 miles. OS Map Landranger series 139 Birmingham and surrounding area (GR: SP 019726).

New roads and motorways have seared across this part of Worcestershire so close to Birmingham. But at Withybed Green is a little oasis of peace with some pretty countryside (although there is no sign of the withies (willows) which were used for basket making). The route does cross the M42 twice but we can soon escape again to quiet footpaths.

The Walk

Turn left out of the car park and walk to the end of the cul-de-sac lane. Climb a stile to the meadow then go over another stile to a hill pasture. Walk up the field gradually leaving the left hand border to pass through a metal gate. Maintain the direction along a cart track to buildings which were once a farmstead but have now been converted to dwellings. On the lane turn right to a T junction.

Cross to the signed footpath. Go along the edge of a field and woodlands to a bridge over the motorway. In the field beyond walk to the stile in the bottom left hand corner. Follow the path alongside a garden to a road. Turn left. There is soon a path running alongside the road right. Go under the motorway and rejoin the road.

Continue past a junction to a T junction. Turn right. Within ¼ mile go through a white gate left. Follow the edge of a right hand brook to a corner bridge and stile. Walk alongside a hedge on the right towards a cottage. Here there is a bridleway. Continue left. Follow the bridleway to a lane by a house. Turn left and climb the hill.

Keep ahead at the road junction. After about ¼ mile the next path is signed over a stile left. In the field follow the indicated direction to walk quite soon at the edge of the field. A few steps past a hollow go through a gate to pick up a left hand hedge. Follow the path to the tunnel under the canal.

Continue around the following field to a stile at a crossing place of the railway. Go over the station road to a path to a road. Turn left to the canal bridge. Gain the towing path and walk beside the waterway to the next road bridge. It is here the bargees left their craft to find their refreshment like us at The Crown Inn.

Stoke Pound
The Queen's Head

This is not only a popular pub for walkers and seekers of quiet ways but also for the captains and crews of holiday narrow boats as it is on the bankside of the Birmingham and Worcestershire Canal. It is pleasant to sit in the large lounge and watch the boats (and swans) passing by.

The Giles family of this popular house were uncertain of the origins of the Queen's Head; perhaps it was once a rural cider house and provided fare for the bargees when the canal was a commercial waterway. This stretch was opened in 1815 after 25 years of petulant construction and the nearby Tardebigge flight of locks (vessels climb 220 ft in 2½ miles) is considered the finest in the land. There was a forge nearby no doubt to re-shoe the horses pulling the longboats. Long before the extensions of the pub the building also served as a post office and off licence.

The beers sold include Courages Best Bitter and Directors. There is also John Smith's Yorkshire Bitter, besides a fine selection of ciders including Autumn Gold, Dry Blackthorn and Taunton Red Rock. The choice of food is magnificent but the speciality of the Queen's Head

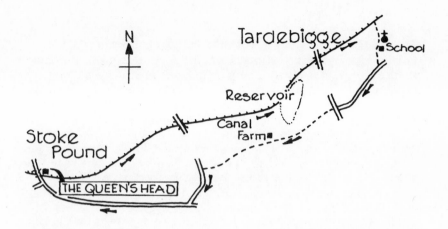

is the carvery so work up a good appetite on the ramble (vegetarians are not forgotten by the way). There is a children's room (they are also allowed in the carvery but not in the bar) and a blind eye is turned towards well-behaved dogs away from the eating area. The children appreciate the fine playground with swings and slide, and a bouncy castle in the summer.

There is a caravan and camping site opposite the pub and pretty gardens in which to sit and watch the world (and those boats) go by. The pub is open from 11 am to 3 pm and from 5 pm to 11 pm.

Telephone: 01527 877777.

How to get there: One mile south of Bromsgrove turn off the A4024 along the lane signed to Stoke Prior. Within a mile Stoke Pound is reached and the Queen's Head is on the left just before the canal bridge. (If coming from Droitwich on the A38 turn onto the A4024 to Bromsgrove and take this same turning, signed to Stoke Prior, after the turning onto the B4091.)

Parking: There is a small car park by the pub and a large main car park a few yards along the lane back to the main road.

Length of the walk: 4 miles. OS Map Landranger series 139 Birmingham and 150 Worcester and the Malverns (GR: SO 961679).

The walk starts by going for a mile or so along the towing path of the canal. With so many locks on the Tardebigge flight it is a gentle climb for the walker but hard work for the boatmen. The top lock is the deepest narrow lock in England with a fall of 14 ft. After a steep climb to the lovely hilltop church of Tardebigge the return route is along a farm cart track and quiet lane.

The Walk

Leaving the car park turn left on the lane and cross the canal. Immediately join the towing path on the left. Walk alongside the canal (now on your left side) and pass many locks. After 1 mile there is a reservoir at the side of the waterway. Shortage of water was always a problem with the necessity of servicing the locks.

After about 2 miles the canal approaches a long tunnel (a length of about ⅓ mile under the hillside). Alongside the garden of a lock-keeper's cottage is a stile to climb to a pasture. Go up the hillside aiming to the right side of the church with the lovely slender 135 ft high spire. St Bartholomew's church at Tardebigge was built in 1777 after the collapse of the old building. (The rather strange name of Tardebigge is from the Saxon 'Tyrde Biegan' – Tower on the Hill.) Through the churchyard a school is reached – I read that in the 18th century this was the site of the Magpie Inn.

Turn right (school now on left) then swing left in the playing field to a stile to a lane. Turn right to a junction of lanes. Cross directly over to a farm cart track and follow this to a lane. Turn left to a T junction and there turn right: The Queen's Head is a little over a mile along the lane.

Abberley
The Manor Arms at Abberley

The Manor Arms at Abberley offers facilities, food and hospitality of the very best. There is a touch of luxury to add to the traditional in this 300 year old pub (originally owned by the Lord of the Manor) but ramblers are made very welcome as well.

The front of the building is decorated with the coats of arms of many local families including the de Todanai, a Norman family during the reign of Edward II. There are two cosy bars (beamed of course) and an inglenook fireplace with the spit racks above. Comfortable though the bars are, you will be tempted to take your drinks on the garden terrace at the back of the pub – the view across the green valley is magnificent and breathtaking. The pub like many rural houses once brewed its own beer but now you will be spoilt with the choice between real ales from Banks's, Bass and Springfield, with the choice of cider resting between Strongbow Dry and the sweet Autumn Gold.

The hours of opening and meals are the normal lunch and evening sessions. The menu is compact but caters for all tastes (with choices for children and vegetarians). Visiting dogs are allowed (except in the dining areas) but will have to make friends with the resident quartet of canines – and the ghost of 'the Grey Lady' if she should appear in the lane outside.

Telephone: 01299 896507.

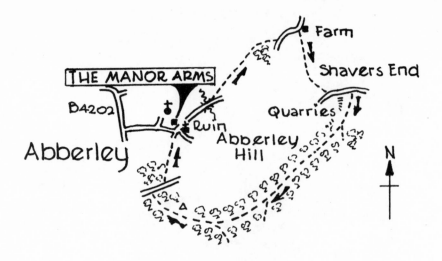

How to get there: The Manor Arms at Abberley is situated in the centre of the village opposite the part-ruined Norman church. The lane to Abberley is off the B4202 ½ mile north of the junction with the A443.

Parking: There is a car park at the rear of the pub.

Length of the walk: 4 miles. OS Map Landranger series 138 Kidderminster and Wyre Forest (GR: SO 753679).

The area of the Abberley Hills with its hanging woods and green vales is great walking countryside but is so beautiful that it is a place to linger awhile. You will be tempted to come again to The Manor Arms at Abberley for a longer stay. The route to 'over the hills and far away' is mostly along the Worcestershire Way and well waymarked.

The Walk
Out of the car park turn left along the lane which drops down to a brook. Immediately over the bridge and by the drive of Crocketts Farm take a signed path over a stile left. Follow the arrowed route at the edge of the pasture above the brook. There are further waymarks to walk below a right hand wood of beech trees that was coppiced in past times to provide the timber for sheep hurdles. Turn 90° right (so the wood is still on the right).

Take care by a pole horse jump as the waymark sign may be missing. Bear left over the field to the far left corner of the pasture. Climb the step stile to a lane. Turn left for 500 yards. By a farm is a bold signpost. Take the signed bridleway to the right along a cart track (marked 'main route'). The track is clear over the fields to climb steeply to a lane. Turn left for ⅓ mile.

Just past a vehicle entrance to a working quarry take a signed foot-path on the right. The path is well trodden (but sometimes a little damp, which means there are giant blackberries in the autumn). Follow the Worcestershire Way signs along wooded tracks through the Abberley Hills. Two especially interesting buildings will be seen in the valley below. There is the tall Gothic clock tower (Jones's Folly) which was built in 1884. A mile or so distant are the ruins of Witley Court – a huge mansion which was gutted by fire in 1937. Near the ruins is Witley church – one of the finest Baroque churches in England. The path goes past a triangulation plinth then twists through trees to a lane. Turn right a few steps and climb a stile left. The route is now clear to a vehicle way. Turn right to The Manor Arms at Abberley.

Ruins of St Michael's Norman church, Abberley.

Hanbury
The Gate Hangs Well

Mark and Louise Giles deserve to succeed – they have taken a rather remote pub (which was once a cider house for agricultural workers) situated along a squeezed country lane where there is little passing trade and turned the place into a most popular venue. They are not frightened of innovation and their ideas create a unique haven and a truly original country pub.

The menu card is a colourful and humorous work of art in the form of a gate that opens to display a modest but varied and well thought-out list of tempting suggestions. I especially commend the duck suppers on selected evenings – 'half a 6lb duck . . . with a home-made orange and Grand Marnier sauce'. The thought of this after walking the route will really quicken your homeward step. There are dishes that will likewise please the vegetarians. (Note the 'groan groan' but fun rhymes on the menu. Mine hosts invite the customers to better them, and win a free meal for two for the best one of the week.)

The beamed bars are attractive with spacious eating areas in the 17th century building and a huge inglenook fireplace. A splendid new addition is the new dining room conservatory which is kept pleasantly

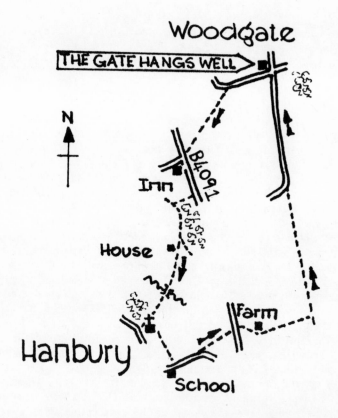

cool in the summer months. There is a wide assortment of real ales –
including M & B, Bass, Worthington and Stone's bitter. We also find
Tennants, Caffreys and Carling Black Label lager. Children are
welcome in the dining area and they have their own 'codling's corner'
on the menu. Opening hours are 12 noon to 2.30 pm and 6 pm
to 11 pm.

Telephone number (to book that duck supper): 01527 821459.

How to get there: Take B4091 south from Bromsgrove. At Stoke Heath
turn left along the lane signed to Woodgate. After 1½ miles the pub
is at the crossroads.

Parking: Park at the pub or along the wide lane if the car park is full.

Length of the walk: 3½ miles. OS Map Landranger series 150 Worcester
and the Malverns (GR: SO 966665).

The walk is through gently undulating countryside, with a few steepish climbs especially to the hilltop church at Hanbury. It is mostly a pastoral farming area but the well waymarked route does pass through the beech woodlands of Piper's Hill – lovely at all seasons but especially at autumntime.

The Walk

From the inn car park turn right along the lane. Pass a farm where you may have to ward off a dozen or so inquisitive but harmless geese. Ignore the first stile and path. Just beyond a yard selling wooden garden furniture is a signed path on the left. This is our route. Follow the indicated direction over the meadow. On the far side we find a reassuring waymark arrow directing us left alongside a hedge. The field is often full of fairy rings – an intriguing mystery.

Over a pole stile and through a railing gate keep ahead to go over a double plank stile – another arrow here to guide us diagonally across a pasture and through a corner gate. A fenced way now leads to the B4091. There is another pretty inn here with an attractive sign depicting a buxom 'Country Girl'. However, you will not yet have worked up a thirst . . . this will come soon with Piper's Hill ahead.

Turn left along the road. Within 400 yards climb a stile to a meadow on the right. Walk alongside the hedge. On a distant horizon are several 'humps'. To the left are Woodbury and Abberley Hills. The poet A.E. Housman gazed at the others and asked 'what are those blue remembered hills?' They are the Clees.

Nearer are the tall radio masts of the famous Droitwich transmitter which for over 50 years has broadcast the BBC's long wave. On a lane turn left to the end. Cross the grass to a cinder path through the woods of Piper's Hill. Join a vehicle drive and pass a renovated farm. Keep ahead soon to pass through a kissing gate and climb the knoll on which is perched a hilltop church. This is St Mary's, Hanbury but locals know it as the Archers' church. Weddings of the radio family have been recorded here.

Take the path out of the churchyard on the far left side of the church. Drop downhill to a lane, with an ancient cross to the right. Turn left for 300 yards. Take a signed path on the left and climb to a road. Cross straight over (but there is the interesting Jinney Ring Craft Centre ¼ mile to the right).

Go down a vehicle drive past a farm (cow sheds now converted skilfully to pretty holiday cottages). Keep ahead through fields to a wide cart track. Turn left. The hill to the right is called Forest Hill which reminds us that these lands were once part of the vast Forest of Feckenham. Maintain the direction at a lane – which leads directly to that 'gate which hangs well'.

36

Feckenham
The Rose and Crown

The Rose and Crown is in what was the main street of Feckenham. Now, sadly, every shop, the post office and the cottage industries of making needles and fishhooks have all gone. There is an old print of the pub in the lounge which shows the stabling and a brougham. This is still a 'horsey' village but now the pub (which once was a favourite for agricultural workers) depends on local trade. It has been a pub for at least 150 years and was a hotel for some time. Paddy McWalter has run this very traditional and comfortable inn for some time – nothing spectacular but a cosy place with open wintertime fires, low beams and many nooks and corners in which to discuss (or forget) the world's problems. Opening hours are from 11 am to 3 pm, and from 6 pm to 11 pm.

The food is classic pub fare and excellent value: ploughman's lunches and home-made pies to accompany the Hanson's and Banks's real ales. Children probably prefer to stay in the rear garden and guard Fido.

Telephone: 01527 892188.

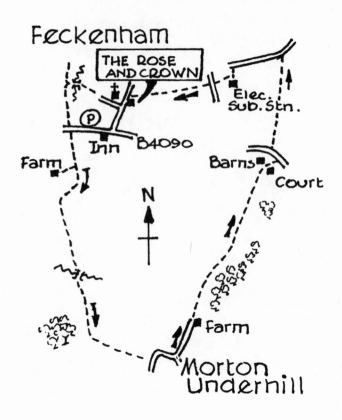

How to get there: The pub is along the main street of Feckenham off the B4090 about 6 miles south-west of Redditch.

Parking: Very limited at the side of the pub but allowed in the street outside. There is a public car park off the B4090.

Length of the walk: 6 miles. OS Map Landranger series 150 Worcester and the Malverns (GR: SP 010616).

The walk is along tracks and paths over an undulating area which was once part of the vast Royal Forest of Feckenham and covered 200 square miles. King John loved to hunt here. The village of Feckenham is a delightful mix of building styles with fine Georgian houses, red-brick, whitewashed and half-timbered.

The Walk

From the pub cross to the green. On the right is the church of John the Baptist. This Norman building has a 13th century tower which houses bells which have been rung for over 300 years. Follow the lane through the green which is signed as a no through road. Walk alongside a sports field which was the site of the royal hunting lodge. Pass a former mill which once 'scoured' the locally made needles. Over the brook is a sometimes muddy area and a junction of tracks. Turn left and follow the track to the B4090.

Cross to the vehicle way opposite which is also a bridleway. The vehicle way bends right to a farm but keep ahead along the bridleway. Follow the way of horses through a metal gate to reach a brook. Turn right to follow the waters downstream to cross a footbridge.

There is a signpost at a junction of tracks. Take the direction shown to Morton Underhill. Climb the rise alongside a left hand hedge and cross horse gallops. Keep on the same heading to reach a cart track then a hedged green road to the hamlet of Morton Underhill. Here is a really 'away from it all' place with just a huddle of cottages, a farmstead or two and a large duckpond.

On the lane turn left and follow this way to the end by Manor Farm – a typical black and white Worcestershire building. Pass the house and continue through gates and the farmyard. Keep ahead alongside a right hand hedge and go through a metal gate. Bear right in the pasture to pick up the border of a high ridge and wood (on the right).

Pass through a bridle gate in the far corner. Keep at the edge of the following field to a metal gate. Follow the direction of a waymark arrow, now aiming towards a hill covered by a new plantation. Keep this on your right to pass through a gate by an oak tree.

Pick up a well-used bridleway at the edge of trees and cross a brook. Continue at the side of a pasture, pass a horse jump and go through a metal hunting gate. Walk towards a magnificent 16th century house called Shurnock Court. Pass through a bridlegate by the moat and keep at the side of the meadow to turn through a corner gate.

Continue by farm buildings to the B4090. Turn left. Cross to the layby where a bridleway is signed. In the fields climb up the steep Wheating Hill then walk at the edge of the ridge and continue to a road. Turn left for ⅓ mile. Turn left down the drive of an electricity station. Within a few yards climb a stile on the right to a sheep pasture. Walk by the left hand hedge to a lane and cross it. Go alongside the hedge then keep the heading across the next field and stay on the direction to the road near the Rose and Crown.

Inkberrow
The Old Bull

The Old Bull is said to be the most painted pub in the country. Besides its most picturesque appearance the place has received fame as the Archers' hostelry – it is said The Bull at Ambridge was based on The Old Bull and many admirers of the radio family come here.

The half-timbered black and white building nestles in a hollow just off the village green. It started life about 400 years ago as a farrier's shop selling saddlery and harness for horses – this is why the beams are so high in part of the bar. Later the owner began brewing his own beer and the place soon developed into the village alehouse. Legend has it that Shakespeare stayed here on the way to collect his wedding ring or marriage certificate at Worcester. Another tale told is of tunnels to the vicarage where Charles I slept after the Battle of Worcester.

This is a pub full of character and interest. There is one bar (mostly flag-floored) but many cosy corners and the place is full of fascinating bric-a-brac: old agricultural tools, photos of the Archers and regimental plaques.

The opening hours are 11 am to 3 pm and 5.30 pm to 11 pm. The real ales available are Castle Eden, Wadworth's 6X and Boddingtons with Blackthorn cider on draught. The extensive menu is displayed on a blackboard and always contains a good assortment of salads, omelettes and filled jacket potatoes. Dogs do not mind staying outside – so Nell tells me.

Telephone: 01386 792428.

How to get there: The Old Bull is on the A422 Worcester to Alcester road at Inkberrow 5 miles west of Alcester.

Parking: In the pub's own car park.

Length of the walk: 5 miles. OS Map Landranger series 150 Worcester and the Malverns (GR: SP 014572).

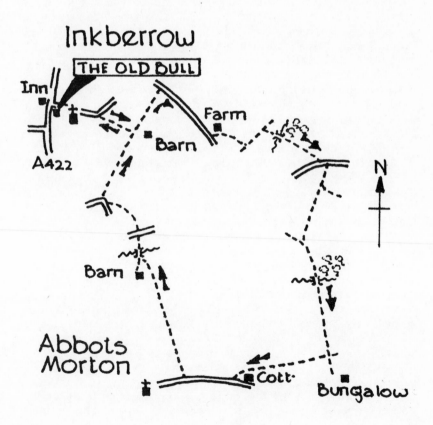

There is a gentle rolling countryside around Inkberrow. With such a mixed terrain of arable and dairy farming and several woods the scenery is constantly changing and interesting.

The Walk

Out of the car park turn right along the lane past the church. The lane drops down to a junction. Go almost straight over through a gate and along a cart track. Keep at the edge of arable fields alongside a hedge. By a barn climb a fence stile and turn left by a left hand hedge. Pass through a field gate and keep ahead to a lane. Turn right.

Fine views now of the Malverns, Bredon and the Cotswolds. Immediately past Lench Farm climb a rather hidden fence stile left. In the field go in a diagonal direction passing an electricity post to a wide hedge gap. Maintain the heading to a fence stile to a bridleway.

Continue left to pass through a gateway and 200 yards beyond turn right – a wide way over a ditch by an oak. Cross the field making for the right hand corner of a wood. Here is a new bridge over Piddle Brook. Proceed by the left hand wood then through a corner metal gate. Keep the direction at the side of pines then follow a way to a lane. Turn left then right along a signed bridleway.

Within 200 yards the vehicle way twists sharp left. Keep the old heading passing through a metal gate and beside a left hand hedge. Go through a corner gate and maintain the direction to a corner hunting gate somewhat overgrown beyond. Keep ahead to join a well-used bridleway, muddy after rain. Do not despair – it does clear. There is a left hand wood then an arable field with a bungalow in the corner. Look for a path going 90° right through bushes. Climb a wired up gate to an arable field. Walk straight down to a rough stile then keep the bearing by a left hand hedge. Just past a cottage gain the road and turn right to the lovely village of Abbot's Morton.

After 300 yards and by converted barns take a signed footpath along a vehicle way right. Past a house called Wood Blewit climb a step stile. Follow the fenced vehicle way and when this bears sharp right keep ahead through a gateway to walk alongside a left hand hedge.

Go over a corner fence stile to keep by left hedges. Pass through a corner gap. Keep ahead. A few yards to the right of the next corner go over a footbridge. Climb the rise picking up a right hand hedge to a stile to a farm drive. Turn right to a lane. Cross to the opposite stile and path. In the field walk away from the lane to a stile. Turn left alongside the hedge to a wide corner gap. Drop down to Appletree Lane. At once take a signed bridleway right. Pass a bijou thatched cottage and keep on the bridleway to the original route by a barn. Turn left over the fence stile and retrace your steps to The Old Bull.

Hadley Heath
The Hadley Bowling Green Inn

A fascinating thing about our English country pubs is the multitude of features for which they achieve fame. This inn (besides being popular because of the fare offered) is proud that there has been a bowling green alongside for over 400 years. It is said that some of the Gunpowder Plot conspirators met here. The inn dates from about the same time as the green and much of the original stout timberwork can still be seen. The proprietor, Tony Richards, is more recent, having come over from Australia and so liked the place that he bought it. He seems to love us 'poms' too but still insists on flying the Aussie flag.

The menu is quite the most extensive I have found and is constantly changing. Prices are very reasonable – and when I called there was a free home-made sweet if you timed your walk to order an evening meal before 7 pm. Opening hours are 12 noon to 11 pm, meal hours being from 12 noon to 2 pm and 6 pm to 9.30 pm (10 pm Friday and Saturday). Beers are Banks's, Hook Norton, Marston's and guest ales.

Working dogs still come with their masters from the fields and do not object to visitors sharing their local. There are no special facilities for children except children's favourite meals.

Telephone: 01905 620294.

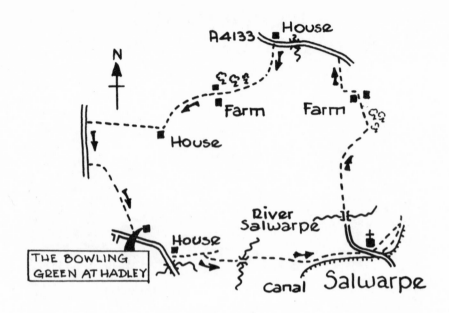

How to get there: The inn is just off the A449 (lane signed Hadley) or the A4133 (signed Ladywood) 3 miles west of Droitwich.

Parking: There is a large car park.

Length of the walk: 3½ miles. OS Map Landranger series 150 Worcester and the Malverns (GR: SO 862621).

The walk is over gentle countryside with no steep climbs. It starts along the valley of the little river Salwarpe – the river of salt. In the same valley is the Droitwich Canal – built to connect the Worcester Canal with the Severn. It is now being restored. There is then a level path to the A4133. The final paths are through mixed farmland.

The Walk

Out of the pub car park turn left along the lane. Within 300 yards take a signed path (Salwarpe) along a vehicle drive on the left. Soon leave the drive – the path is indicated down the bank to the right. The way is a little overgrown in places but the twisting way is passable. The line of the path may be lost for a few yards but climb the ridge ahead from where you will then see the bridge to cross the river Salwarpe. At once climb the fence stile. Follow the arrowed direction to go through the meadow to a far step stile. Here is another arrowed direction to follow. The path continues to a stile to join the canal towing path. Walk alongside the water and pass under a long bridge where ivy hangs low. A few hundred yards beyond the bridge take a path left. Somewhat double back (waterway now on left) to follow a path to a churchyard.

This is Salwarpe church (built in the 14th century on earlier foundations). Follow the path to a lane. Turn right. The cottages nearby were once a school then a shop. Keep ahead at the end of the lane to cross the river then follow a cart track beside mainly arable fields.

Go through a white gate to parkland. Still follow the faint line of the cart track. Do not go through the far white gate (through which a ghostly carriage is said to journey from High Park to the church) but bear left. Pass through a gate and walk by farm buildings (some converted). Continue along the vehicle way ahead to a field. Follow the edge left to the A4133. We have had glimpses of a magnificent brick-turreted house. Westward Park is from Tudor times and was begun in 1592. Turn left for ½ mile. This is a busy road so do take care. Almost opposite cottages and on the brow of a hill take an unsigned path left. Go through a gate and in the field walk alongside a left hand hedge. Turn the far corner to the right and go through a gate by a wood. Follow the cart track past a farmstead to a lane. Turn left for 400 yards. Take a signed path left. Walk alongside a hedge for a few steps. Climb a stile and follow the arrowed way back to the inn. If you have a little energy left you can have a game of bowls.

Berrow Green
The Admiral Rodney

Although far from the coast The Admiral Rodney maintains the nautical connection, from the boat washed up and abandoned on the front lawn to the names of the three bars and the decor. Jim Gunter the owner of this free house insists that the Worcestershire Way actually goes through the bars. Many travellers along this long distance county pathway have reason to appreciate the warm welcome at the strategically sited hostelry.

The earliest record of an inn here dates from 1640 and it is thought that Rodney had his country seat in Worcestershire. The real ales offered three centuries or so later at this free house are Hook Norton, Enville Bitter and two different guest beers each week. This is a real old fashioned inn which likes to see walkers (even with muddy boots) and dogs (even with muddy paws). There are often parties of ramblers who set off from their coach some miles distant to tackle a section of 'The Way' to end at the Rodney.

The food offered is standard pub fare but the portions satisfy the well-earned appetites of walkers and the home-made soup by open fires is especially popular on winter hikes. Children are welcomed

with smaller-sized meal portions and there is a large grassed play area (where tents can be pitched). The pub is open from 11 am to 3 pm, and 7 pm to 11 pm.
Telephone: 01886 821375.

How to get there: The Admiral Rodney is on the B4197 road 5 miles south of Great Witley.

Parking: There is a large car park in front of the pub.

Length of the walk: 3 ¼ miles. OS Map Landranger series 150 Worcester and the Malverns (GR: SO 747586).

This walk is through the interesting undulating countryside above the valley of the river Teme. There are some magnificent viewpoints along the route – hills do have to be climbed first though! There are also meandering paths through woodlands – here are some of the most attractive sections of the Worcestershire Way.

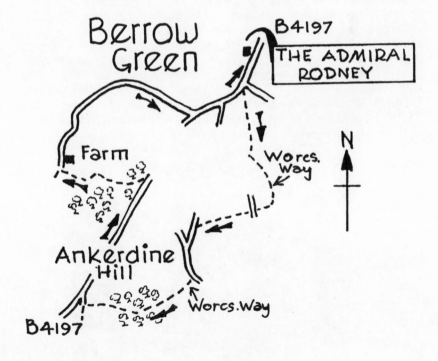

The Walk

Out of the car park of The Admiral Rodney turn right along the B4197. After a few hundred yards and just past a junction take a signed path left. We are now on the Worcestershire Way which follows a route through the county from Kingsford Country Park in the north to near the Malvern ridge in the south. Follow the directions clearly indicating the path which is waymarked over stiles and through fields. The marking is either yellow arrows or WW signs to a lane. The next path is directly opposite over a stile by a gate. Cross a field to a metal gate. Maintain the heading across a pasture to a stile which is about 100 yards to the right of the distant gate.

There is now a pretty view with the summit of Ankerdine Hill to the right and the Malvern ridge on a far horizon away to the left. Turn left on a lane and go past a junction and farmsteads. Look for the next path signed through a metal gate right. In the pasture continue by a left hand hedge to descend a steep hill to a wood. Swing right (still in the field) to a hunting gate and follow the clear winding track through the trees. The route is marked by yellow arrows and ignore side turnings to reach a pasture. Climb this to a vehicle way. Turn right to the B4197 and go right again to the summit of Ankerdine Hill.

Keep on the road for about ¾ mile. Opposite a house drive turn left along an unsigned path downhill through woodlands. Out of the trees, descend through a rough hill pasture (more woods on the left). Go through a gap and continue on a grassy track alongside large fruit trees with woodlands still away to the left. Pass through a gate with double chain and keep descending to a cart track. Turn right past farms to the B4197. Follow the road for ¼ mile, The Admiral Rodney is to the left.

Dunhampstead
The Firs Inn

The Firs is situated some 3 miles from any A or B road. John and Suzanne Kearney in this free house have had to ensure that the journey of customers is worthwhile to travel along winding country lanes. How well they have succeeded is obvious if you visit during lunchtimes or evenings.

The pub (probably built as a house in the last century) is between a railway line and canal – a lonely spot where nightingales sing in the woods nearby. The garden is bursting with flowers in summertime and there are pretty views over the fields from the lounge windows. The rooms too are tastefully decorated with garden blooms. It is a fine place indeed in which to relax after tackling the route.

The choice of meals is really daunting – one is spoilt for choice from the menu but in addition there are several boards on which are chalked, bistro-style, the many specials of the day. I particularly liked the beef steak in a rich Guinness, cider and mushroom sauce and for Sunday lunch there are at least two roasts on the menu. Vegetarians and children are not forgotten in the culinary delights. Another board states the enticing sweets – how about raspberry pavlova or summer pudding?

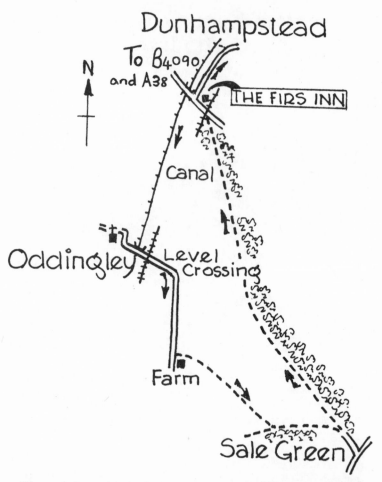

The real ales sold are M & B and Banks's Bitter and the draught cider is Taunton Dry Blackthorn. Hours of opening are 11.45 am to 2.30 pm and 6.15 pm to 11 pm but all day opening applies in summertime. Children are allowed but the house dogs – Elsa, the German shepherd, and Tara, the labrador cross – advise other dogs to stay outside.
Telephone: 01905 774094.

How to get there: From the A38 1 mile south of Droitwich turn left and follow lanes signed Dunhampstead for about 3 miles.

Parking: There is a large car park alongside the pub.

Length of the walk: 4 miles. OS Map Landranger series 150 Worcester and the Malverns (GR: SO 918600).

Here is a ramble which will delight those who find the stillness of a quiet waterway so therapeutic. I have taken a little detour at the start of the walk to see where the canal enters a tunnel. Later the route is alongside extensive woods where the remoteness encourages many species. There are no hills on the way – but the Firs menu will give you an appetite.

The Walk

From the car park turn right on the lane to the canal. Turn right along the lane. Within 500 yards the lane twists sharp right. We go left, then within 100 yards or so take a path on the left to the towing path. The canal was completed in 1815 (24 years after it was authorised). The original cost had been estimated at £180,000 but the final cost was over three times this amount. Here the waterway goes through a 35 yard long tunnel. Follow the canal for a mile to a road bridge. This is at a scattered hamlet called Oddingley. You will see the little church with a 17th century tower. In 1806 the parson was murdered by a local carpenter.

On the lane turn left to cross the railway at a level crossing. This is a rarity these days as although this is a busy line the gates are controlled manually. After ½ mile along the lane and immediately before a farm take a signed bridleway through a gate on the left. Follow the way of horses to a wood.

The track follows alongside the trees (now on your right side) towards the hamlet of Sale Green. By the houses and wood there is a path going left and this is our way. The path hugs Trench Wood for a mile then keeps ahead to recross the railway near the Firs Inn at Dunhampstead.

Lower Broadheath
The Dew Drop Inn

This is an inn which seems to exude warmth and fun, with plenty of pub games, happy hours and quizzes. There is an 'It's a knockout' contest in the summer and children have a wealth of garden contraptions on which to play (making me wish I was young again). Thirsty ramblers too find a ready welcome. The building was not originally built as a pub but as a south-orientated doctor's house – hence it does not face the road.

Lesley Barnett is only the fifth landlord of this Marston's pub in 60 years. She supplies real ales – Marston's Bitter and a guest beer and a good selection of ciders. Meals are traditional pub fare and there are 'small portions for small people'.

Nell was given a fine welcome too and I was assured this was the 'norm' for well-behaved dogs. Opening hours are 12 noon to 3 pm and 6 pm to 11 pm but flexible hours are the rule in the summer months.

Telephone: 01905 641774.

How to get there: From Worcester cross the river and go along the A443. After a mile turn left along the B4204. On entering the village go left. The Dew Drop Inn is ½ mile on the right.

Parking: There is a large car park alongside the pub.

Length of the walk: 3½ miles. OS Map Landranger series 150 Worcester and the Malverns (GR: SO 807564).

This is a walk through the gentle countryside that Elgar knew. He was born in a cottage at Upper Broadheath which is passed on the route. (A fascinating museum is open daily.) There are no steep hills to climb and the walk ends across commonland.

The Walk

The start of the walk is over a stile at the back of the garden and children's play area. On a vehicle drive turn right but immediately leave it again. By the gate to Jassamine Cottage climb a stile and follow the fenced way at the side of gardens. Keep the direction over a stile to a pasture and continue at the sides of fields to the road (B4204).

Turn right and go past a road junction (another pub here). Stay on the B4204 for a further 300 yards. Take a signed bridleway up a slope left and through a gate. In sheep pastures walk by the right hand border to a lane. Cross directly over and walk through fields to a vehicle way. Turn right to the main road.

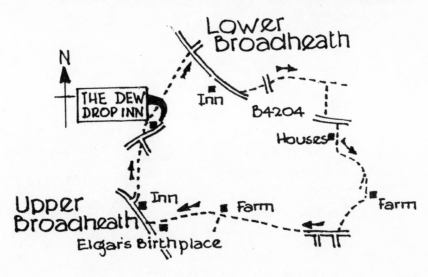

Cross the road and continue left for 200 yards. Turn right down a signed bridlepath. Near houses keep ahead through a metal bridlegate and proceed along a well-used track alongside a hedge. Turn left by a little water works.

The farm cart track bears right but soon leave it to pass through a bridlegate left to a meadow. Walk the length of the field towards an old farmhouse. Just before the building turn right over a fence stile by a barn. Through rough ground climb over a step stile to a farm vehicle drive and continue along this to a road.

Turn right and keep ahead when the road becomes a farm cart track. Continue to a farmstead. Keep on the same direction through a bridlegate. Walk along a house drive then maintain the bearing through a further bridlegate.

The farm cart track goes over lovely countryside to the road by the little cottage where Elgar was born. Turn right for 300 yards then right along Laycock's Lane. This is a cul-de-sac and at the end maintain the direction over the common to a road by a junction. The Dew Drop Inn is a few steps to the right.

Longley Green
The Nelson

This free house pub is hidden in a valley below the Suckley Hills – these are gentle uplands where orchards thrive on the slopes facing the sun. The building dates from around the early 17th century and it has been a hostelry for around 200 years. Now Bill and Maralyn Christie are building up a reputation for good meals and well-kept real ales. The range of food is modest but Maralyn is proud of her home-made specialities (including vegetarian fare) and the eight or nine desserts are really irresistible after walking a few miles.

Banks's and Boddingtons beers are the standards but there is always a guest beer which is changed each week. Cider addicts have the difficult choice between Weston's Scrumpy, GL and Strongbow. 'Well-behaved children are warmly welcome' says the menu and with a family themselves the Christies know what children with a healthy appetite like. Outside there are plenty of benches and tables and a play area with some exciting looking gadgets. Dogs are welcome except in the dining areas (where incidentally the old well is a feature).

Opening hours are from 12 noon to 3 pm, 7 pm to 11 pm.
Telephone: 01886 884530.

How to get there: Turn off the A4103 3½ miles west of Worcester. Follow lanes via Leigh and Alfrick to Longley Green.

Parking: Park in the pub's large car park.

Length of the walk: 5 miles. OS Map Landranger series 149 Hereford and 150 Worcester and the Malverns (GR: SO 732503).

The walk starts along the valley of the fast-flowing Leigh Brook which races eagerly to join the river Teme. There follows a stretch through lovely woodlands (wellies or boots advisable). Before the village of Alfrick (where there is a church with distinctive wood shingles) you can explore the 63 acres of The Knapp Nature Reserve. Along some delightful squeezed lanes the route climbs steeply to the viewpoint of Crews Hill. Here the Worcestershire Way is joined and this leads us over Suckley Hills back to The Nelson.

The Walk

Out of the car park turn right along the lane. Take the left fork at a junction. We go past the large black and white house of Tundridge – so typical of the Worcestershire countryside. Within a mile and immediately before Mousehole Bridge climb a fence stile on the right. Walk down the pasture near the right hand wood. Go through a gate and climb a clear track alongside the woods. At the top of the slope go through a barrier and continue along the pathway just inside the woods.

Follow the well-used path keeping close to the left hand brook. Past an isolated cottage join the vehicle drive. The wide way goes past a nature reserve and twists an attractive way through the trees. When you reach a lane, follow it to a T junction. Turn left to The Knapp Nature Reserve. Almost opposite take a farm road which becomes a rough track and climbs a rocky way. At the top of the steep slope pass a farm and continue to a lane at Alfrick.

Turn left and keep ahead at junctions to follow signs to Crews Hill. Just over the brow take a path signed Worcestershire Way on the left. There are plenty of waymark arrows to keep you on the route but look out for a sharp turn right to drop down to a lane.

Cross directly over to walk alongside orchards before plunging into woodlands. Again follow Worcestershire Way signs. Emerging from the trees climb a stile to a rough hill pasture. Drop to the gate in the right hand corner. Cross horse gallops and walk along the path to a lane. The Nelson is to the right.

Leigh Sinton
The New Inn

Although on a main road this pub is strategically placed for walkers as the Worcestershire Way runs alongside and it is surrounded by some magnificent undulating countryside. John and Linda Horsley took over a rather run-down inn (originally built as a house for a smallholding) and a challenge to build up the reputation. That they have succeeded is obvious – besides the well-presented real ales (Marston's Best Bitter and Banks's Mild) and traditional pub fare at very reasonable prices – including vegetarian dishes – the Horsleys have won an award for their lovely garden each year.

My collie Nell did not object to being excluded from the bar – this is also the rule for children but there is a fine grassy play area. At the side of the New Inn, and owned by the brewery, is an ancient hay meadow on which there is a conservation order. Here there are cowslips in abundance and rare orchids – orchis morio and gymnadenia conopsea, I'm told.

Opening hours are varied according to the season but note that bar meals are only available lunchtime (12 noon to 2 pm).

Telephone: 01886 832353.

How to get there: The pub is on the A4103 6 miles south west of Worcester.

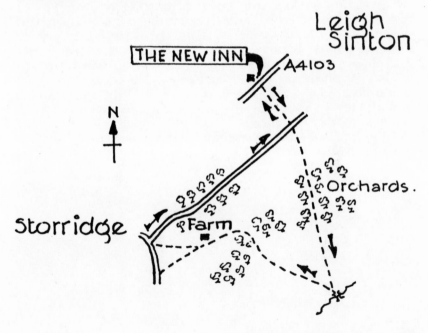

Parking: There is a car park at the front of the pub.

Length of the walk: 3 miles. OS Map Landranger series 150 Worcester and the Malverns (GR: SO 760494).

North of the Malvern ridge is pleasant undulating countryside where many of the slopes are covered in orchards. Hops were once grown in abundance and oast houses are a feature of the countryside. There are several cider makers in the area and one cider farm is strategically placed on the route.

The Walk

From the pub car park cross the road and take the signposted route (Worcestershire Way) down a vehicle drive. Climb a stile by a gate and keep ahead alongside a left hand hedge to meet a lane. Cross directly over maintaining the direction still by left hand borders of fields. In a far corner go over a bridge (often no water below) to an orchard.

Turn left, then at once right to regain the original heading walking between apple trees. Towering ahead now is North Hill – the first high upland of the Malvern ridge. Out of the orchard keep ahead over the step stile then follow the waymarked route through pastures.

We come to a meandering brook. Do not cross over the bridge but swing sharp right. Go over the rough pastureland to pass just to the right of a line of low bushes to a waymark post. Continue to climb the steep hill alongside an old ditch to a step stile to a wood. Keep ahead to join the vehicle drive and follow this out of the trees. Pass near the ancient black and white farmhouse. The correct line of the path is now to the right off the drive to a lane by a road junction. However, it appears that the preferred route is to stay on the drive to the road and turn right to the junction. Turn right along the lane – a lovely narrow and quiet byway which goes through the woodlands of Crumpton Hill. Descend to the crossing pathway of the outward route. Turn left along the path to return to The New Inn.

Kempsey
The Huntsman

When you visit this free house be pepared to be welcomed by Neil Harris's three hunter horses.

What they pretend to guard is a splendid pub which is situated along a quiet lane near to one of Worcestershire's few commons at Kempsey. The Huntsman (which, strangely, was called The Fox 30 or so years ago) is well known to lovers of fine well-kept real ales – Everards Tiger Bitter, Beacon and Old Original. There is also good cider, Stowford Press from Much Marcle and Scrumpy Jack.

This is a village pub where chatty friendly conversation is a feature. There is oak furniture, an open fire, rural characters, a skittle alley and horse prints on the walls of the two bars which have many cosy corners. The meals available are written on a blackboard and although the range is not extensive there is good value for money and always a vegetarian dish. The cold table buffet is particularly popular.

Children and dogs are welcome at The Huntsman and there is a play area and benches and tables in the garden. Hours of opening are 12 noon to 2.30 pm and 5.30 pm to 11 pm.

Telephone: 01905 820336.

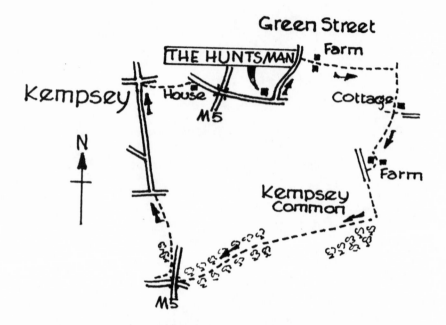

How to get there: From the centre of Kempsey village on the A38 south of Worcester turn eastwards along Post Office Lane. Go over a crossroads (pub signed) and the motorway bridge. The Huntsman is 300 yards beyond on the left.

Parking: There is a large car park at the side of the pub.

Length of the walk: 4 miles. OS Map Landranger series 150 Worcester and the Malverns (GR: SO 869491).

There are few hills on this walk – just a gradual climb to the plateau of Kempsey Common. This is a large area of open grass with gentle views over the Severn Valley and Worcester. The M5 motorway is never far from the route – the walker can see the traffic racing past – and retreat thankfully to the quiet byways.

The Walk

From the car park turn left, then at once left again at the road junction along a lane signed to Hatfield. Within ¼ mile take a signed bridleway along the drive of Woodhall Farm on the right. Keep ahead past the white farmhouse and along a wide hedged track. Pass through a metal gate and maintain the heading at the side of a field.

A few yards through the next gateway (no gate) pass through a metal bridlegate. Resume the old direction but now by a right hand hedge. Continue up the field to turn right through another bridlegate. There is now a well-used track along the ridge which gives good views of the Malvern Hills.

Near a cottage pass through metal gates to maintain the heading along a signed pathway. Walk at the border of a field to a farm. The line of the path is well waymarked with yellow arrows between barns to the left and to a lane. Turn left, then pass through a gate to Kempsey Common. Continue to the far side of the grass. Turn 90° right and gradually leave the left hand border of the common.

Aim towards some distant tall trees. Pass through bushes to reach the trees and maintain the direction near the left hand border of the now-wooded common. Follow the clear track which wends a way through the trees to a lane. Turn right under the motorway. The next path is on the right. Either go over a stile (if reinstated) or pass through a gate to the field. The next path runs alongside the motorway.

Keep by the highway passing into the next field. Within a few steps enter woods and follow a well-trodden path through the trees so gradually leaving the side of the motorway to reach a road. Cross to the lane almost opposite. Keep ahead at the next junction to a crossroads. Take a signed path to the right. Follow the direction indicated. Pass the end of a hedge and keep ahead to pass through a metal gate. Now aiming towards a house walk to a gate to a road. Turn right over the motorway bridge to The Huntsman.

Bishampton
The Dolphin

There is nothing grand or pretentious about The Dolphin but it is a simple village inn with a warm welcome and something different in pub grub. Ray and his wife, Denise, have been in the pub trade for over ten years. Previously they had been in city pubs but now enjoy the country life and especially the garden. Ray and Denise are building up a reputation for the choice and quality of their beers and food. The pub has been refurbished and with the renowned cooking from Denise's kitchen (pies are a speciality) ramblers are most welcome.

The history of the inn is somewhat obscure. I am uncertain as to the claim of it being a coaching inn as it does not seem to have been on a main highway, but undoubtedly there was a considerable horse trade here with extensive stabling and a resident blacksmith. The name was once The Fish and the story goes that it changed to The Dolphin with local associations with the French Dauphin. Again I have my doubts, although descendants of the French royal family certainly lived at Wood Norton only a mile or so distant.

Ray and Denise have been in the licensed trade for many years so know how to present well conditioned real ales, the choice being between Bass Traditional Bitter, Ruddles and Worthington. In addition Carling Black Label, Fosters, Kronenbourg and Pilsner lager are also on draught. There are two rooms – the lounge and the bar. Children also have use of a games room and are allowed in the bar. There are plenty of benches and tables outside. Being a country inn, dogs are part of the scene and have been known to have guided some merry customers home. The opening hours are 12 noon to 3 pm and 6 pm to 11 pm.

Telephone: 01386 462215.

How to get there: About halfway along the A422 Alcester to Worcester road, turn along the lanes southwards signed to Bishampton for 3 miles. The pub is in the centre of the village.

Parking: There is a large car park behind the pub.

Length of the walk: 6 miles. OS Map Landranger series 150 Worcester and the Malverns (GR: SO/SP 989515).

The walk starts in flat countryside of mixed farmlands and climbs to some lovely hills around the villages called the Lenches. Here there are fine woods and upland sheep pastures. The lanes used are attractive and carry little traffic and part of the route is the long distance path – the Wychavon Way.

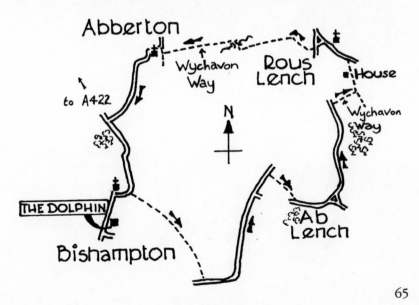

The Walk

Leaving the car park turn right to walk through the village. The road swings right near the church of St Peter (mainly 19th century but with parts from the 12th). At the end of the village take a signed bridleway on the right and follow the well-used track to a lane.

Turn left. Just past a junction and opposite a farm drive go along a signed bridleway through a gate on the right. Walk at the edge of the field to climb the ridge. Pass through a bridlegate to a lane. Turn left. Follow the lane to the hamlet of Ab Lench. (Was this once Abbots Lench? – the area once belonged to the Abbot of Evesham.)

At the village green take the lane left – signed to Rous Lench. Within ¾ mile look for a footpath on the right. It is signed as the Wychavon Way with a crown emblem. Walk at the left edge of sheep pastures keeping ahead. When the Wychavon Way is signed 90° right in a corner turn left over a step stile. Walk through an orchard and along a drive to a lane. Turn left to Rous Lench passing the little church which has Saxon and Norman work.

At the green bear left. Just past a farm take a signed bridleway on the right. This is again the Wychavon Way. Follow the many waymarking signs to take a route over a brook and at the edge of fields to a T junction of tracks. Turn right along the vehicle way to a lane at Abberton. Turn left to pass the church which had its spire 'lopped' in the 1950s because it was in line with the runway at Pershore airfield. At a T junction turn left to Bishampton and The Dolphin.

Great Malvern
The Wyche Inn

The Wyche Inn must have one of the finest views of any pub in the country. From its site high on the side of the Malvern Hills you can gaze far across the vale of the river Severn towards the Cotswolds. The temptation must be to cancel the walk and feast on the view (and the delicious fare offered by Ralph Palmer). This free house was on the ancient salt route but has only been a pub for around 150 years. Elgar found inspiration for some of his loveliest music when he walked and cycled over the Malverns and some say he quenched his thirst at this pub.

The appearance inside is most attractive, with many potted plants – and of course one is keen to sit on the 'patio with the view' if the weather is kind. The menu of home-made food always includes four vegetarian dishes, the spicy vegetable crumble almost tempting me to change the habit of a meat-eating lifetime. There is a daily chef's special displayed on a blackboard with the mouthwatering sweets, the favourite of which when I called being Malvern Hills blackberry and apple pie.

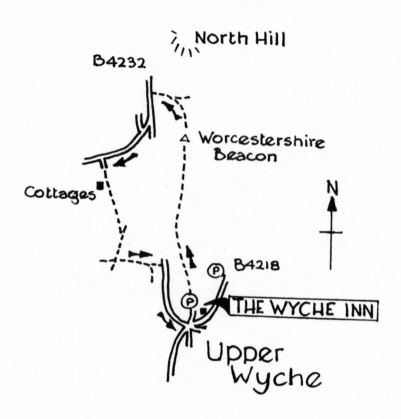

The real ales – Ruddles and Webster's – are well kept and draught Fosters is also available. Opening hours are 12 noon to 3 pm and 7 pm to 11 pm.

There are seven en suite rooms available (with that view a free extra of course). Well-behaved children are welcome as are dogs (away from the eating areas).

Telephone: 01684 575396.

How to get there: The Wyche Inn is on the B4218. Turn off the A449 to the right from Great Malvern. It is on the right just before the Wyche cutting near Upper Colwall.

Parking: There is a small car park at the side of the pub or a large Malvern Conservators public car park further down the hill.

Length of the walk: 3½ miles. OS Map Landranger series 150 Worcester and the Malverns (GR: SO 769437).

The Malvern Hills are invigorating uplands for walking. They have inspired artists, poets and men of music providing wide and lovely views over the old counties of Worcestershire on one side and Herefordshire on the other. The first part of the walk is the puffing climb up the Worcestershire Beacon. There was a tearoom at the summit – at 1394 ft the highest point in the county and an ancient signalling station – until it was destroyed by fire a year or so ago . . . which makes the pub visit even more attractive.

The Walk

From the pub, climb along the B4218 and go through the Wyche cutting where the rocks (some of the oldest in the land) are exposed. At a junction of roads turn right – signed Beacon Road. This soon goes through car parking areas and becomes a twisting way which gradually climbs uphill. At the summit is the triangulation plinth and a monument to commemorate the Jubilee of Victoria's reign in 1897.

Walk down the steep slope. Ahead is the lofty North Hill. There are signs to St Anns Well reminding us of the Malvern Spa Water which has been famous for its medicinal properties since the 18th century (because said Dr John Wall it was . . . 'containing just nothing at all').

Do not start climbing North Hill but turn left – the way is signed to the Dingle. We join a tarmac way which leads to the B4232. Turn left, then after a few hundred yards go right down Harcourt Road. Within ½ mile turn left down a vehicle way. At the end are cottages. Walk through a gate and through fields to a stile to a rough vehicle track.

Turn right. There is a crossing track after 300 yards. Turn left. Go past cottages. By a green the vehicle track twists sharp right. Keep ahead over the grass then climb to a stile onto the B4232. Turn right to the Wyche cutting and the Wyche Inn.

Wyre Piddle
The Anchor Inn

This is a pub that regularly finds its way, and with ample justification, into 'good pub' guides. The lessees of this Whitbread's house are Michael and Scarlett Senior and, as Michael was once the chef of one of the top large hotels in the area, it is no surprise to see the delights on offer both in the two bars and the cosy beamed restaurant.

The home-made products are served with vegetables which are collected daily from the Vale of Evesham growers just down the road. Vegetarians are far from being forgotten and their 'specials' are always included on the blackboard bill of fare at the bar (try the vegetable Dauphinoise!). There is a good array of real ales with Flowers Original, Boddingtons, Marston Pedigree and IPA available with a guest beer which changes every 2 weeks. Castle Eden being especially good when I called.

The bars are particularly friendly in this 400 year old building. There are interesting old prints on the walls, darts evenings open to everyone, a splendid inglenook fireplace and magnificent views across the river Avon (which runs alongside the pub garden at the rear). 'We are pleased to welcome children', says the notice and there would have been a similar statement for Fido (and Nell) if they could have read it. The pub dogs Charlie, the retriever, and the lovable Heinz 57 called Tilly appreciate visitors to their home.

This fine pub is open from 11 am to 2.30 pm and 6 pm to 11 pm. Telephone: 01386 552799.

How to get there: The Anchor Inn is situated in the middle of Wyre Piddle on the B4084 between Pershore and Evesham.

Parking: There is a small car park alongside the pub and additional streetside parking off the main road.

Length of the walk: 4 miles. OS Map Landranger series 150 Worcester and the Malverns (GR: SO 965475).

There are no hills on this walk, the route is in the flat valley of the river Avon over market garden lands, but we have many distant views of uplands – the Malverns, Edge Hill and Abberley Hill. Fladbury, a river village with a magnificent mill and weir and a 15th century church, is visited.

The Walk

Turn right out of the car park and walk along the B4084. Within ¼ mile go down Chapel Lane on the right. After a couple of steps two paths are signed. Take the right hand way signed to Lower Moor. Pass through a white gate by a house called Nait. Follow a well-cleared hedged track to a stile to a vehicle way. Cross directly over – the path is signed.

Continue along the wide track to a meeting of ways. Go right a step or two then regain the former direction through willow trees and over

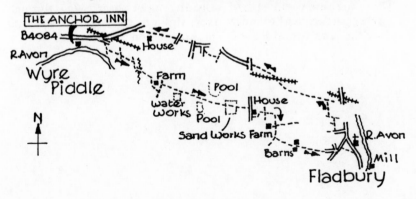

a brook. The path goes to the left of a pool to a market garden field.

Walk to the right of greenhouses. By the farm swing right then left to go to the right of a Dutch barn. Pass through a hedge gap to a farm drive. Turn left, then right – the path is signed 'Fladbury'. Keep a fenced water works compound on your right to pick up a wide farm 'road' still maintaining much the same direction. Go between pools and past buildings of a small sand and gravel establishment. Walk along the drive to a lane by cottages. Turn right a few steps then take a path left. The path goes around the garden of a cottage to a field. Turn right and continue with a hedge now on your right side.

Cross a farm track and follow the well-used path around a wood and farm (keep on right) to a farm drive. Cross to the signed path along a cart track opposite. Within 200 yards there is a meeting of tracks. Turn left (left hand hedge) to farm buildings. Pass between the buildings to regain the heading (right hand hedge). Nearing houses pick up a lane and continue to a junction. Turn left (Farm Street). Within 200 yards take the signed path on the right to the centre of Fladbury. Turn left along Church Street then Station Road for a few steps. Proceed left down Coach Drive. By new buildings turn right. The path is not signed down a vehicle way alongside left hand allotments.

When the vehicle way swings left keep ahead alongside a wooden fence and gardens. At the very end is a T junction. Turn left then at once right. The path is signed at the back of gardens to a farm vehicle way. Turn left, then keep ahead at a footpath to a crossing place of a railway. On the far side turn left to a lane. Cross directly over (Blacksmith Lane). By Anvil Cottage the road twists right. Turn left along a cart track. Within 100 yards the footpath branches off right. Keep along this way to a lane. Turn right then left at a T junction for 100 yards.

Cross the lane to the signed footpath (Upper Moor). Walk through a market garden field to a cart track. Cross to the opposite stile and follow the path to the B4084. The Anchor Inn is to the left.

Cleeve Prior
The King's Arms

The history of the King's Arms is a little obscure although it has obviously been in existence for many centuries, as is evidenced by the ancient pigeon loft. A book published 100 years ago mentioned 'hundreds of pigeon holes'. There are cosy bars where the beams are dated 1542. The landlord takes great pride in the quality of his beers (Flowers Original, and Boddingtons compete with several guest beers). Food is available daily from 12 noon to 2 pm and from 7 pm to 9.30 pm. Mrs Boswell is proud to state that here (no doubt to satisfy the large appetites after tackling the walk) one can obtain 'the best chips in Worcestershire' and Sunday lunches 'just like mother makes'. I especially liked the help-yourself salad bar.

Children are welcome and there is a garden in which to use up that surplus energy. Nell my border collie appreciated the bowl of water offered without her having to ask and fully understood that she was not allowed into the dining room.

The pub is open from 11.30 am to 2.30 pm and from 6.30 pm to 11 pm.

Telephone: 01789 773335.

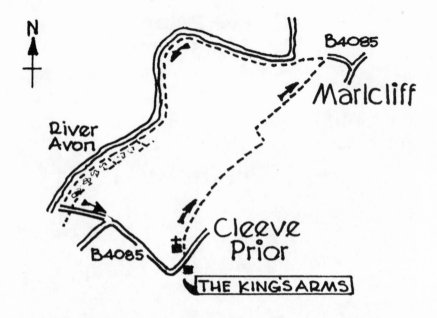

How to get there: The King's Arms is in the main street of Cleeve Prior. Approach the village along the B4085 2 miles south of Bidford-on-Avon.

Parking: Park in the car park behind the inn.

Length of the walk: 3¼ miles. OS Map Landranger series 150 Worcester and the Malverns (GR: SP 088493).

Cleeve Prior is situated on a long ridge above Shakespeare's river Avon. There are therefore gentle views across the valley for the outward leg of the walk to Marlcliff. Homewards is along the riverside path, so in the summer months you can pass the time of day with the captains and crews of the holiday craft. The only steep climb to accentuate your thirst is the final lane up to Cleeve Prior.

The Walk
Opposite the inn take the path signed to Marlcliff. Go down the vehicle drive (Curate's House on left) to a gate to a churchyard. The church of St Andrew has work of Norman masons and on the tower buttress are marks where arrows cut from the 600 year old yew were sharpened. Keep the church on the left to a gap between two tall trees to a meadow.

74

Climb a stile and pass by a huge chestnut tree (prize winning conkers in season). To the right is Cleeve Mánor, where Thomas Bushell hid after supplying Charles I with money when he lost the Royal Mint. Maintain the heading through a field of thistles that would make a Scot sigh for his homeland. Into the next fields still maintain the same direction now alongside left hand hedges, then a right hand hedge over a step stile.

In a corner turn left for 150 yards to a wide hedge gap then resume the former heading to pass through lines of apple trees. Cross a sometimes arable field to a stile to a meadow. Climb another stile in the far left hand corner. Pick up a left hand hedge. The distant village is Bidford – 'Drunken Bidford' to Shakespeare, who so loved the taverns there.

Over another stile bear slightly right to drop down steeply through bushes to a gate to the hamlet of Marlcliff by a toytown cottage capped with thatch. Turn left along a vehicle drive signed as a bridleway. Pass a cottage with a lovely garden (open to the public on selected days). Follow a path which borders the tranquil Avon to the site of the former quay and mill to find Mill Lane going left. At certain seasons the path through the woodlands can be a little overgrown. You have the option of several unmarked paths up the steep slope left to a wide vehicle way. Turn right from this to Mill Lane.

Mill Lane passes (on right) a nature reserve (established in 1983 to protect wildlife on the unique ridge) and leads to the B4085. Cleeve Prior and the King's Arms are to the left.

Hanley Swan
The Swan

The situation of The Swan is wonderful – it borders the trim village green at Hanley Swan (so called to distinguish the place from Hanley Castle a few miles distant). Crowning the green is a huge billowing oak and across the road is the lily pond where ducks (if not swans) glide. There were once three inns in this tiny village but although everyone agreed that it was old (the building dating back about 400 years) the history of The Swan seems a little obscure. It is the pub for countryfolk and an established gathering place for local people. The bar is carpeted so do watch those muddy boots!

This Whitbread house has a reputation for its welcoming atmosphere and the good home-made fare offered. I especially liked the pies and the menu (if not extensive) caters well for hungry walkers. Children's meals are available and youngsters love the large play area with swings and climbing frames.

There is a good selection of beers with both Flowers and Theakston's real ales, and cider drinkers can choose from a selection including Taunton and Blackthorn. Opening hours are 12 noon to 3 pm and 6.30 pm to 11 pm. Sorry Fido (and Nell) – you stay outside.
Telephone: 01684 310639.

How to get there: The Swan is by the crossroads at Hanley Swan on the B4209, midway between Malvern Wells and Upton upon Severn.

Parking: There is a car park behind the pub.

Length of the walk: 4½ miles. OS Map Landranger series 150 Worcester and the Malverns (GR: SO 813429).

What is particularly attractive on this walk is that always we are within sight of the towering Malvern ridge. On the route, however, the terrain is quite flat through pastoral and arable farmlands (sturdy footwear advisable after rain).

The Walk

Opposite the inn take the footpath signed to Ox Hill. This is along a vehicle way which soon becomes a farm cart track. Cross a brook by Home Farm. Keep ahead at junctions of tracks – a way signed to Stable Farm. By the elegant white farmhouse stay on the same heading.

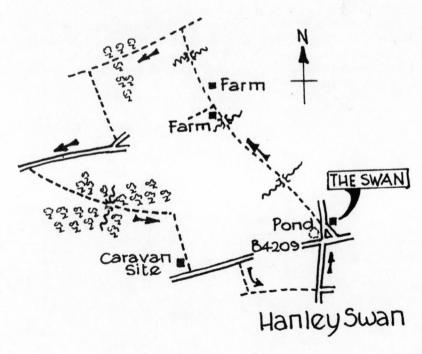

Climb a step stile to the left of barns and walk along a tractor way alongside a right hand wire fence. Go through a metal gate by a brook and maintain the direction up a grassy hill – a modest slope but what a magnificent view at the little summit, with Bredon Hill on a distant horizon.

Go over a stile then cross a horse gallop to another high stile. Immediately over turn left, with a seat nearby to rest awhile. We are now on a snake-like track which wends a way through bushes. (I hope I am not giving secrets away when I say there are fine blackberries to be picked here at autumntime.)

Through a gate we enter woodlands – still the track is well-walked – then through bushes. Over a step stile in the corner of a field turn left alongside the hedge to a corner gate. Keep on the same direction to a vehicle way. Turn right to pass former military buildings. About 400 yards past a tall water tower climb a step stile on the left.

Go alongside a hedge (first on right then left) to walk soon at the border of left hand woods. Continue to a far corner of the fields to a stile to enter woodlands. Cross a brook and walk through the trees. Climb a stile to a field and maintain the direction aiming towards a low electricity pole. Climb a stile by a metal gate to a cart track. Turn right. Follow the way past a caravan site to the B4209.

Turn left. Within 400 yards and by the village sign turn right through a metal gate. Walk directly away from the road beside the fence to a corner gateway. Turn left through the gate and walk at the top of a pasture to a gate to a vehicle drive. Follow this to a road. Turn left to the green at Hanley Swan and the pub.

Hanley Castle
The Three Kings

Here is a very picturesque 15th century 'village' pub tucked in a corner of the little green at Hanley Castle. There are three flagstone-floored small rooms for walkers who only want to quench their thirst. They are full of atmosphere – and the drinks are served through a hatch. The furniture of high settles, spindle-back chairs and simple wooden stools is just right – as is the huge inglenook fireplace which takes up one complete wall.

Pub games like darts and cribbage are enthusiastically played and morris dancers energetically jingle their bells outside in summertime. There is a fair chance they try the beer too . . . and what a choice in this free house, run by Mrs Sheila Roberts and her family for many years (it has been in the family for 80). Besides the regular real ales of Thwaites and Butcombe there are always a good variety of guest beers stated on a board over the bar. When I called there was some strong stuff . . . I found Cotleigh Tawny and Fuller's London Pride (both OG 1040) and Greene King Abbot Ale (1049). For cider drinkers there is Weston's Scrumpy and Dry Blackthorn – and folk singing on Sundays.

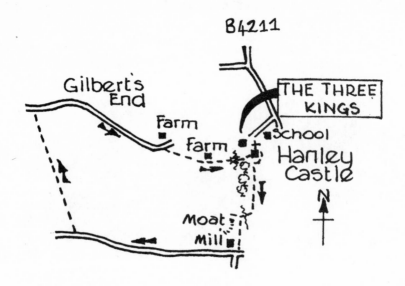

The carpeted lounge is called Nell's Bar – no, my border collie has not been honoured – it was the cottage of a lady called Nell before it was acquired by the pub. The very cosy (and more modern) room is entered by a separate door. Here the selection of the home-cooked food is very wide. We find the traditional fare such as soups, sandwiches, steaks and omelettes but the more adventurous (and patient as the wait may be up to ½ hour) can try such delicacies as chicken or salmon en croute or beef Wellington. Vegetarians are not forgotten – how about a Provençale nut Wellington?

The hours when the pleasures of this delightful hostelry can be tried are 11 am to 3 pm and 7 pm to 11 pm. There is bed and breakfast too – ideal when testing those strong beers. Perhaps not an ideal pub for children, but they are allowed in a side room. Dogs – I should take the advice of the house dog called Buster and stay outside and admire the view.

Telephone: 01684 592686.

How to get there: 1½ miles north of Upton upon Severn along the B4211 the pub (and Hanley Castle) are signed down a cul-de-sac lane on the left.

Parking: Limited around the green at Hanley Castle.

Length of the walk: 3½ miles. OS Map Landranger series 150 Worcester and the Malverns (GR: SO 839420).

The land around the inn is quite flat in the vale of the Severn but there are some nice footpaths and twisting and interesting lanes. Always on the walk we are in sight of the Malverns. There are plenty of attractive black and white cottages hereabouts and ancient farmsteads.

The Walk

Take the signed path near the inn to enter the churchyard of St Mary's church. This is a magnificent building of mellowed brick set in place in 1674. Follow a way to keep immediately left of the church then turn the corner to the porch right.

Walk directly away from the porch to the far corner of the churchyard. Pass through a metal kissing gate. Walk alongside the hedge (on left) of the churchyard to an arable field and along the border at the edge of a wood. Within 300 yards twist right to rough ground then regain the former heading now walking along a clear winding track to another kissing gate.

Go right to climb a step-stile and cross a brook. Climb another stile. A few yards further go through a metal gate and left along a grassy track. We are now bordering a moat. This once surrounded the castle of Hanley Castle and was no doubt fed by the nearby brook.

Pass through a metal gate and walk along a vehicle drive of a mill which has been converted to a house. On a lane turn right. After 1¼ miles take a farm track on the right. It is immediately before overhead power lines and is signed as a footpath. The wide track leads to a lane. Turn right through the hamlet of Gilbert's End. After ¾ mile take a path over a stile by a gate right. (Warning: the sign says 'Hanley Castle' but may be pointing an incorrect direction.)

Take a heading over the open field passing to the right of an isolated distant oak to a wide hedge gap. Pass through and walk alongside a left hand hedge to a metal kissing gate. Beyond, walk near a farm (on left) and at the edge of fields to pass through a rough hunting gate to an arable field. Maintain the heading (or walk around the edge) to a metal bridge.

Continue through a new plantation and cross a brook. Climb through trees to the outward route to walk through the churchyard to The Three Kings.

Elmley Castle
The Queen Elizabeth

Tony Howells was quite adamant that business was so good 'there is no need to advertise'. In these times this really indicates a pub which has something different. Its position (in the main street of a pretty village clustered below Bredon Hill) and its history (an inn when the first Queen Elizabeth came to Elmley Castle) obviously are assets. However, the landlord then went even further – he serves no meals (unless you can count unusual crisps such as ham and mustard flavour). It transpires that this is a real village hostelry where locals (especially the cricketers) come for the beer (beautifully kept real ale – Marston's Best Bitter) and the bar games (shove-halfpenny, darts and quoits), walkers coming for the no-nonsense welcome (with no strange looks when they unwrap their own sandwiches) – and the beer! There are two cosy bars (open 11.30 am to 3 pm and 7 pm to 11 pm but 'flexible' if cricket is being played) with beams, stone floors and ancient settles. Outside are loads of benches and tables – children are OK here but not inside. Tony's preference for dogs is obvious from the loads of prints on the walls – so Fido will probably be welcomed.

Telephone: 01386 710209.

How to get there: Take lanes signed to Elmley Castle off the A44 west of Evesham. The inn is at the end of the main village street near the church.

Parking: Park at the rear of pub or in the main street.

Length of the walk: 5½ miles, but can easily be shortened. OS Map Landranger series 150 Worcester and the Malverns (GR: SO 983411).

Bredon Hill (beloved by poets) is beautiful walking countryside with magnificent views in all directions. The ramble starts gently through level farmland but soon the climb begins. The route continues through scrubland (where deer roam) and woods to the plateau summit (around 1000 ft). There are flattish paths to the ancient hillfort and folly tower then a spectacular track along the top of an escarpment. The way drops to a lane back to Elmley Castle.

The Walk

Opposite the inn go through the gate to the churchyard. Keep to the left of the tower of the Norman church of St Mary which has many monuments inside to the Savage family, old lords of the manor. Pass

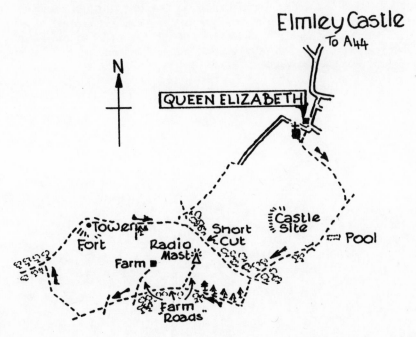

a pool and look down on a lovely garden. Follow a clear way over a stile to a field. Continue to another, then follow the edge of a field (right hand borders). Away to the right is the knoll on which the castle of Elmley was perched until it became a ruin by the early 1400s.

Proceed to a plank bridge and stile which you must cross. Bear left in a meadow to follow, and never far from, the left hand fence to a distant pole stile. Cross a stream and turn right through a metal gate. Pick up the yellow crown signs of the Wychavon Way.

Keep ahead, then past a left hand pool swing right over a wide bridge. The waymarked route now goes between trees and through rough pasture to a gate to scrubland. Continue climbing through woodlands. Out of the trees on the plateau summit is a junction of tracks. Go right then at once left through a gate (but keep ahead by right hand woods for a short cut). Follow alongside isolated pine trees for 400 yards. Turn right, still by pines. Keep ahead by woods on the left. Pick up a tarmac way, with a radio mast away to the right, then cross a tarmac farm drive. Go past one junction of signed paths. Four hundred yards further take a path to the right over fields to a bridleway through woods. Turn right. Pursue the path past folly tower, large stones (folklore associations) and hummocks of hillfort. Follow the edge of the escarpment through a gate, by a pine wood to more woods. Turn left, then right along a clear track through the trees. Cross other tracks to descend soon through bushes. Go through a gate into rough hill pastures. Walk near the right hand border to join a farm cart track. Turn right through gates to a lane. This leads to the Queen Elizabeth at Elmley Castle.

Ashton under Hill
The Star Inn

The 400 year old Star Inn at Ashton under Hill once had to compete with The Plough and Harrow and The White Hart but these were long ago converted to private houses. Nowadays The Star on its own serves well the pretty village nestling under the eastern slopes of the splendid walking upland of Bredon Hill.

With its cosy welcoming interior (warm blue carpets and furnishings) and a growing reputation for good value home-made meals this Trent Taverns pub makes a good place to end a walk. It is often featured in magazine articles and pub good food guides – the pies prepared on the premises especially appealed to a hungry walker like me. Children are particularly welcome with small tempting portions and even high chairs if required. But please keep Fido (although his manners may be impeccable) in the garden where there are plenty of benches and tables to guard.

The real ales available are Theakstons XB and Best Bitter and Boddingtons Bitter augmented with keg Flowers and Boddingtons. The main cider sold is Dry Blackthorn. I rather like the idea too of a piano singsong by the open fire in the beamed bars after a winter

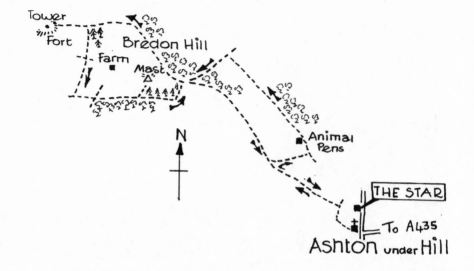

walk, or of partaking in the garden barbecue in the warmer seasons. (I almost forgot to mention that vegetarians are not overlooked – there is usually a choice between three dishes).

Opening hours are from 11.30 am to 2.30 pm and from 6 pm to 11 pm.

Telephone: 01386 881325.

How to get there: About halfway between Evesham and Tewkesbury turn off the A435 along the lane signed to Ashton under Hill. Turn right at the T junction by the church. The Star is a few yards along the road on the left.

Parking: There are car parks behind the pub and opposite.

Length of the walk: 7 miles. OS Map Landranger series 150 Worcester and the Malverns (GR: SO 378997).

The start of the walk is a stiff climb up the lower slopes of Bredon Hill (immortalised in A.E. Housman's poem 'Summertime on Bredon') and along the waymarked path through Worcestershire called the Wychavon Way. At the furthest point on the route are several interesting features – the large ancient hillfort, the folly tower (which took the height of the hill above the magical 1000 ft mark) and rocks around which tales of folklore are woven.

86

The Walk

From the pub walk down the road to the church. Go into the churchyard and keep to the left of the church. Walk through a kissing gate to a meadow and continue to the far right hand corner. Go over a wooden then a stone stile to a vehicle track. Turn right for 200 yards then by a cattle grid climb another stile on the left.

Follow the arrowed route (Wychavon Way) to walk up the field passing a waymark post to a stile. Maintain the heading to the very far end of the 'plateau' field. Climb the stile and keep much the same direction through fields to a large rough hill pasture. Bear right (not quite the arrowed bearing) to pass through a metal gate. Keep ahead a few yards. Here leave the Wychavon Way by going to the right – a signed bridleway marked by a blue arrow along a farm track. Pass through a gate and, bearing right, drop downhill.

Walk through meadowland to join a track which has come from the right. Turn left along this track to pass animal shelters (on your left side). Through a gate keep ahead to pick up the side of extensive woods. Keep these on your right. Go through a hunting gate by a metal gate and stay by the woods. When the woods end keep the old direction to cross a little rivulet. Pass through gates by animal pens. Pick up a tractor way and climb the rise alongside a left hand wire fence. Pass through a gate and bear left. Over the brow of the hill there is a view of the knoll on which Elmley's castle was perched. Drop down to a fence stile. A few steps further turn 90° left now again walking along the Wychavon Way. Pass through a hunting gate then through woods. Follow the clear waymarked route through tall trees to the top of the ridge. For a shorter walk turn left. Otherwise turn right. Keep by the right hand woods, then through a gate follow the path along the ridgetop with a wire fence and fields on your left side. By a little fir wood (on left side) go through a gate and continue to the hillfort and the folly tower. Retrace steps to the fir wood. Do not go through the gate but turn right alongside a left hand stone wall.

Maintain the heading to cross a cart track. Keep ahead to a meeting of signed tracks. Turn left to a hard farm road and cross it. Walk alongside a right hand wood along another farm road. When this swings sharp left to a large radio tower keep ahead (another right hand wood now). Continue by a row of fir trees then follow these around to the left to pass through gates to a track by woods where the shorter route started.

Turn right alongside left hand woodlands, where you may see herds of deer. Follow the clear Wychavon Way route, soon dropping downhill through fields to meet the outward route. Retrace your steps through the churchyard to the road. Turn left to The Star.

Conderton
The Yew Tree

The yew that nudges the pub is a protected tree and has witnessed the change a couple of centuries or so ago from farmhouse to a place that is welcoming to locals and travellers (which includes walkers). The latter should not be deterred by the photo of one in the stocks: 'The last rambler who did not take off his boots'. The building dates from about 1650 and was a favourite cider house opening at five in the morning for the farm workers on the high hill of Bredon which rises from the hamlet.

Shaun and Sally Hickey can justly take pride in the reputation of their free house for offering well-kept beers and good home-made bar snacks. They offer Banks's, Wadworth 6X and Marston's real ales ('the best Marston's Pedigree in the country') and also Grolsch lager on draught. The cider is a choice between Weston's Scrumpy and Stowford Press.

Children have a play area in the garden – they can keep an eye on Fido (and my Nell) as dogs are not allowed in the cosy pub (which is stone-flagged with open fires, a fascinating winding staircase and an ancient bread oven).

The opening hours are 12 noon to 3 pm and 6 pm to 11 pm. By the way, rambling parties are welcome.

Telephone: 01386 725364.

How to get there: 6 miles from Evesham turn off the A435 Evesham to Cheltenham road to the right. Go through Beckford village. Conderton is a further 1½ miles along the lane.

Parking: Very limited outside pub otherwise in lane alongside.

Length of the walk: 4 miles. OS Map Landranger series 150 Worcester and the Malverns (GR: SO 967377).

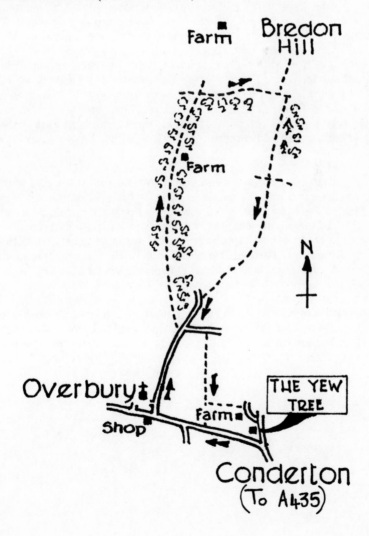

The walk is along the lane to the village of Overbury with its lovely Norman church and the Court – a magnificent mansion built in 1730. There is then an energetic walk up the slopes of Bredon Hill, the reward at the top being of course a splendid view. The descent is alongside woodlands and arable lands.

The Walk

Out of the little car park turn right along the road signed to Overbury. There are no shops in Conderton but we pass country craftsmen such as a potter and a fine silk printer. At a junction (old toll house here) keep ahead to Overbury. Opposite the village shop (lovely ices sold) take the lane on the right, from where there is soon a good view of the Court and church to the left.

Within a ⅓ mile and just before a road junction take a vehicle drive to parkland left over a cattle grid. Follow the vehicle way which gradually climbs uphill to pass farmsteads. By woods is a meeting of vehicle ways. One ahead is to an isolated farm but we follow the tarmac way right. As the tarmac way twists sharp left to radio masts keep ahead on the old direction for a few steps along a sandy cart track.

Turn right through a hunting gate. Walk along a rough grassy track with a wall on your right side and woods on the left. At the end of the trees go through a gate. Keep descending (right hand wall) at the edge of a field to a gate to a cart track. Cross over to walk alongside a wall.

Follow the clear path which keeps woods on the right and is marked by stiles to reach a lane by cottages. Keep the same general direction to a road junction. Turn left for about 200 yards. Take a signed path on the right. Keep a constant heading through farmland. Over the hill pick up the side of a left hand wood. In the corner of an arable field go left into the woods.

After about 40 yards of the winding track go left over a step stile to a field. Cross to a stile to an orchard. Keep ahead to climb a stone stile to a lane. We are now back at Conderton and the Yew Tree Inn is to the right.

Bretforton
The Fleece Inn

There are many unusual and fascinating things about The Fleece, foremost of these being that it is the only pub in the care of the National Trust. The place dates from the 14th century, when it was built as a medieval farmhouse, but it only became a licensed premises in 1848 (recent as pubs go). Farmer Henry Byrd sold beer and cider from his home, a tradition continued to 1977 by his great-granddaughter, Lola Taplin. When she died the place was left to the National Trust on condition it was run as an unspoilt country pub. So visit the pub today and it has the furniture, ornaments and appearance of a 19th century home. There are very many interesting items but especial mention should be made of the 17th century pewter collection, said to be the finest after that in the British Museum.

The present licensee is Norman Griffiths who points out that, although the menu is modest in range and price, to preserve the unique character of The Fleece it is impossible to extend the kitchen facilities and some delay is inevitable – but I can vouch it is well worth the wait. A wide variety of beers and real ales are available including Hook Norton Best Bitter, Hogshead by Uley and others especially brewed for the pub. Weston's Scrumpy Cider is recommended.

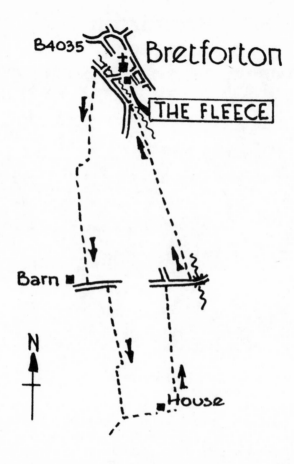

The treasure box that is The Fleece is open 11 am to 2.30 pm and 6 pm to 11 pm (meals 12 noon to 2 pm and 7 pm to 9.15 pm). Children can eat in the pub (children's portions available) but some difficulty may be experienced in dragging them away from the splendid toys in the pretty garden. Dogs could also protest – they are not allowed inside or outside.

Telephone: 01386 831173.

How to get there: The Fleece is situated by the church in the centre of Bretforton just off the B4035 3 miles east of Evesham.

Parking: Park in the public square (called The Cross) outside the pub.

Length of the walk: 3 miles. OS Map Landranger series 150 Worcester and the Malverns (GR: SP 093438).

The countryside around Bretforton is the Vale of Evesham – quite flat with extensive market garden farms. On the walk you will therefore have distant views of many hills – Bredon and the Cotswolds – without having to climb them. The return leg is alongside a meandering brook.

The Walk

From the car park go along Bridge Street with the church on the right. The church is Norman with a tower from the 15th century. Go over the bridge and turn right at the T junction for 300 yards. The first path is signed on the left by a cottage. Go through the gate and keep ahead over a field. (Note the ridges and furrows of the ancient strip farming.) Climb a stile to the next meadow. Walk alongside the left hand border fence.

In a corner go through a hedge gap and climb a fence stile. Again walk by a left border. Turn the far corner to dog leg right then left to regain the old heading by a hedge offering lush blackberries at autumntime. In the next corner take another dog leg to climb a pole stile with waymark arrows to show the direction to emerge on a lane well to the left of a barn.

Turn left then immediately right – the path is indicated down a farm track. Within ⅓ mile skirt around a clump of willows. Beyond is a little problem as the path is blocked with wire. Get through where you can. Pick up a right hand hedge to a vehicle drive. Turn left to keep a house on the left. Just over a cattle grid turn left to go along the vehicle drive to a lane. Turn right. Just before a brook take the signed path left. The path chases the waters downstream to a lane to Bretforton. You may have to wait a little while at The Fleece so you have a chance to keep an eye on the rocking chair – a ghost is said to get it moving.

Broadway
The Crown and Trumpet

The village of Broadway vies for the title of the 'prettiest village in England'. Other folk may have different contenders as far as the village goes, but what is indisputable is that the Crown and Trumpet offers some of the prettiest old-fashioned hospitality. The place still has the feel of the pubs of old with smoothed long settles, massive beams, horse tackle, a piano and log fires but with a discreet addition of 1990s comfort and cosiness – just the place to visit after a walk up the lovely limestone hills above the village.

The hills have been sheeplands for many hundreds of years and, whereas the inns in Broadway's main street served the stagecoach trade, the Crown and Trumpet (and the former other two pubs in Church Street) would have been used by the agricultural workers over the centuries. Pub games like darts and quoits are popular.

Andrew Scott is the lessee of this 17th century Flowers house and has built up a reputation for finely kept beers (Flowers and Boddingtons real ales, including Boddingtons Mild, which is quite rare outside its Manchester base). There are also guest beers – Old Speckled Hen from Morlands sounds interesting. Andrew also prides

himself on his meal menu at modest prices displayed on a blackboard
– there is both standard fare and seasonally varied home-made local
dishes. When I called I found Evesham Pie – a delicious concoction
of beef with plums and the Vale of Evesham asparagus flan.

Children are rarely adventurous with food and they have a separate
menu at the Crown and Trumpet – not quite chips with everything,
not with the special tempting puds, at least. Well-behaved dogs are
accepted at Andrew's discretion. Opening hours are 11 am to 3 pm
and 5 pm to 11 pm, and meals are served as late as possible.

Parties (with ramblers especially welcome) can be catered for and
there are four rooms for overnight accommodation.

Telephone: 01386 853202.

How to get there: The pub is a few yards along Church Street (the road
to Snowshill) from the A44 at the west end of Broadway.

Parking: Limited at the front of the pub but public car park nearby.

Length of the walk: 5 miles. OS Map Landranger series 150 Worcester
and the Malverns (GR: SP 095374).

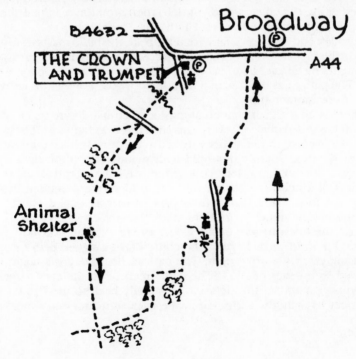

At Broadway Worcestershire nudges the Cotswolds and the walk climbs high above the village. The hills were once almost solely sheeplands but during the Second World War skilled farming produced good arable crops. There are also woodland sections and the walk ends along Broadway's famed pretty main street.

The Walk

From the car park walk along the road towards Snowshill. We pass St Michael's church which was built in 1839 because Broadway's old church was a mile distant. A few steps further cross the road to go down a vehicle drive signed as a footpath. Within 200 yards the path is through a kissing gate. Take the arrowed direction over a pasture then cross a clear sparkling brook. Follow the well-used track to the corner of the next field and a lane. Opposite two paths are signed. Take the left hand one to maintain the old direction along a fenced way to a large hill pasture.

Climb the path to the high wood and go through a hunting gate. The twisting path goes through coppiced trees, these beeches having been cut near the ground to provide a supply of branches for sheep hurdles. The track goes through another gate to a field. The well-used path is signed along the edge (woods on left) then around an animal shelter (keep it on your right side) to a farm cart track.

Turn left and away on a far bare hilltop are the radio masts of Cleeve Hill – the highest point of the Cotswolds. The straight cart track goes through a metal gate by a hay barn. Take the path signed over a stile left. The path hugs the side of a right hand wood. Follow the arrowed path over another stile.

There is now a gentle climb alongside a left hand wire fence. On a distant hill is Broadway Tower. This structure was built in 1798 by the Earl of Coventry to please his wife. Turn corners, still keeping by the fence. We drop sharply downhill with woodlands to the right.

Over a stile turn 90° left. Follow the waymarked path around the borders of a field to a corner stile and bridge over a hidden brook. Continue to a road. Turn left to pass Broadway's 'old' church. St Eadburgha's has much work fashioned by the Norman masons. There is soon the fine gateway of the Court where Charles I stayed.

Five hundred yards beyond the church take a signed path through a kissing gate by a drive right. The path to Broadway is straight and marked by a series of stiles. The path emerges on the main street of the village. You can turn left and dilly dally back to the Crown and Trumpet by window shopping in the fascinating antique shops.

96